AF552508

MICROTEACHING AND PROSPECTIVE TEACHERS

By

Majeti Jaya Lakshmi

M.Sc., M.Ed.

Lecturer, College of Education

Guntur, Andhra Pradesh

Editor

Dr. Digumarti Bhaskara Rao

M.Sc., M.A., M.A., M.Ed., Ph.D.

Reader & Research Director

R.V.R. College of Education

Srinivasa Nagar Colony

Guntur – 522006, A.P.

DISCOVERY PUBLISHING HOUSE PVT. LTD.

NEW DELHI-110 002

Reprint: 2018

First Published-2009

ISBN 978-81-8356-375-8

Published by

DISCOVERY PUBLISHING HOUSE PVT. LTD.

4831/24, Ansari Road, Prahlad Street
Darya Ganj, New Delhi-110002 (India)
Phone: 23279245 • Fax: 91-11-23253475
E-mail: dphbooks@rediffmail.com
dphtemp@indiatimes.com
website: www.discoverypublishing.com

Printed at:

Dynamic Printers, Delhi

Dedicated

to

Mr. Chandra Raveendra

Mrs. Chandra (Akkineni) Atchamamba

In Appreciation of Their

Public Service

Preface

Microteaching is a scaled-down, simulated teaching encounter designed for the training of both pre-serve and in-service teachers. It is a training procedure aiming at simplifying the complexities of regular teaching process. It is also a training technique where a teacher practices with a small group of 5 to 10 pupils for a brief duration of 5 to 10 minutes before peers and mentors on a selected concept of lesson and concentrates on a single skill which is practiced.

Microteaching is a teaching laboratory in which small groups of practicing teachers, faculty and facilitators explore the process of teaching and learning by alternately teaching and responding as learners. The practitioners learn from feedback on their own teaching, from being student while others teach, and from the conversations about these experiences. The basic premise of microteaching is that there are many different ways to be an effective teacher and that the practicing teachers can expand their effectiveness by observing other teaching styles and strategies and by discussing shared issues of teaching and learning, no matter their discipline, unique style, or years of experience.

The present study is intended to find out the attitude of prospective teachers towards microteaching. The prospective teachers studying in Colleges of Education are with a high level of attitude towards microteaching. Except gender, the locality, the teaching methodology, the medium of instruction and the qualification of prospective teachers did not show any significant influence on the level of attitude of prospective teachers towards microteaching.

This study would be of great help to teacher educators, teacher education planners and administrators and heads of teacher education institutions in devising teacher education programmes and in making teacher education courses effective and useful in actual classroom situations.

Dr. Digumarti Bhaskara Rao
digumartibhaskararao@rediffmail.com

Sri Sai Soudha
D-43, S.V.N. Colony
Guntur 522006
A.P., (India)

Contents

Preface

1. INTRODUCTION 1
Statement of the Problem
Need of the Study
Scope of the Study
Objectives of the Study
Educational Implications of the Study

2. REVIEW OF RELATED LITERATURE 10
Theoretical Perspectives
Meaning of Microteaching
Why Microteaching?
How to Micro-teach?
What to Prepare?
The New Microteaching Simplified
Materials for Microteaching
Characteristics of Microteaching
Assumptions of Microteaching
Microteaching and Traditional Teaching
Objectives of Microteaching in College of Education
Procedure of Microteaching
Model of Microteaching
Principles Underlying in Microteaching
Microteaching and Teaching Skills
Modern Categories of Basic Skills in Teaching
Role of Supervisor in Microteaching
Evaluation Instruments

Aids and Apparatus in Microteaching
Advantages of Microteaching
Limitations of Microteaching
Improvement of Microteaching
Guidelines for Preparation of Microteaching
Teaching Follows Talk About Microteaching
Research Studies
Microteaching and Feedback
Microteaching and Self Concept
Microteaching and Personality
Microteaching and Intelligence
Microteaching and Teaching Skills
Microteaching and Locality
Microteaching and Qualifications
Microteaching and Gender
Microteaching and Teaching Methodology
Microteaching and Block Teaching Practice
Microteaching and Effectiveness of Microteaching
Microteaching and Anxiety
Microteaching and Achievement
Microteaching and Teaching Competence
Microteaching and Modelling
Microteaching and Attitude
Microteaching and Direct or Indirect Behaviour
Microteaching and Verbal Behaviour
Microteaching and Classroom Behaviour
Microteaching and Teacher Behaviour
3. RESEARCH METHODOLOGY 120
Operational Definitions of Key Terms
Variables of the Study
Hypotheses of the Study
Sample of the Study
Tool of the Study

4. **ANALYSIS OF DATA** **127**
Data Analysis and Findings

5. **SUMMARY, CONCLUSIONS, DISCUSSION AND SUGGESIONS** **133**
Summary
Conclusions and Discussion
Suggestions for Further Research

BIBLIOGRAPHY ***140***

INDEX ***169***

1

Introduction

The quality of education depends on the quality of teachers. The quality of teachers much depends on the way in which they had received the type of teacher education through teacher education institutions. If our teachers are going to shape the destiny of our country, the teacher education has to assume a great responsibility and has to take recourse to some innovative and effective techniques of educating pre-service and in-service teachers. It was believed that just as the director brings the skill of giving life and form to a movie, so the teacher brings to the teaching-learning situation the skill with which he is able to control and use his teaching exercise and thus influence the other variables of the situation. This skill does not automatically come to the teacher with either a degree or diploma or a teaching contract. Rather, it is a skill developed through the awareness of the interacting elements in a teaching-learning situation, planning strategies for teaching based on this awareness, through the setting of sound objectivities, assessing the results and modifying these objectives in terms of assessment. (Usha Rao)

The traditional teacher education programme (Usha Rao) consists of two major parts: theoretical learning and practice teaching. The theoretical course, which covers philosophical, sociological and psychological foundations of education and the methodology of teaching are chiefly verbal, abstract and vogue. Consequently, they affect cognitive and attitudinal changes rather than behavioural changes in teachers. With regard to practice teaching, it is assumed that, during this period, the pupil teacher will develop proficiency in basic teaching skills and classroom management. In actual practice, however, the programme of student teaching tends to be theoretical and lacks the objective feedback on performance, essential both to motivating and directing behavioural modifications. Hence, improvements were felt to be required not only in theoretical aspect of teacher education curriculum, but also in application of teaching skills.

The entire practice teaching programme fully over shadowed by Herbert's ghost was a subject of criticism. The conventional classroom teaching seemed to be exactly like that of exposing a bride, newly wed, to a strange audience, who neither has the familiarity of place nor the competence. So is the case of these student teachers, who when exposed to the classroom of 70 or 75, neither are capable of showing competency over the content matter nor good effective methodology or teaching. The result is disastrous indeed. The student teacher either entirely withdraws from teaching or remains frustrated for a long time to come. (Usha Rao)

On the basis of the above-said facts, some of the major defects (Usha Rao) of the entire teacher education programme may be quoted, which are as follows:

1. Emphasis of the whole programme is purely on teaching rather than on doing aspect;
2. Classroom instructions are general rather than specific;
3. Number of lessons given by the students teachers is arbitrarily fixed and not need-based or ability-based;
4. Units chosen during practice teaching by student teacher are not continuous and very little scope existed for developing any initiative or dynamism;
5. There is no provision for any sort of continuous or integrated assessment of student teachers;
6. Feedback given to the student teachers about their performance is either subjective in nature or vogue;
7. Supervision of lesson of the student teachers done by method masters is unscientific;

8. Entire practice teaching programme was not suited to individual talent development;
9. There exists no relationship or relevance between theoretical teaching and practical skill of teaching;
10. There is no uniformity in the programme followed in the various aspects of student teaching;
11. Majority of student teachers develop an unfavourable attitude towards practice teaching;
12. Evaluation practices of class teaching range from purely internal to purely external;
13. Number of lessons given by student teachers is arbitrarily fixed and is not based on the needs and abilities of student teachers;
14. There is no clear-cut evidence to say that the present-day teacher education is effective;
15. Teacher educators themselves are not clear about the objectives of teacher education and evaluation procedures to show the extent of their achievement;
16. Supervision of practice teaching lesson is haphazard and indiscriminate and also mostly subjective in nature;
17. Orientation programme before initiating student teachers into practice teaching is, too, inadequate;
18. Further, there is no agreement as regards the total number of lessons to be given by student teachers and the total time spent on practice teaching.

To overcome these drawbacks of the practice teaching programme and thereby to encourage properly the practice teaching programme, a new way emerged and that is called microteaching. Thus, the need to find out a proper solution for removing the defaults in the existing practice teaching programme was fulfilled by microteaching and it emerged on the scene of teacher education with a view to solve the varied problems.

Microteaching

As a scientific approach, microteaching emerged effectively in the field of teacher education as a valid and useful method. The term "microteaching" was introduced at Stanford University in 1963 and was developed by the College of Education as an experimental teacher education programme supported by Ford Foundation. It implies micro-element that systematically attempts to simplify the complexities of teaching process. The purpose of microteaching is to give perspective in terms as much practice in teaching as possible under controlled conditions before they begin their teaching practice and/or internship. Microteaching is one of the training techniques under laboratory conditions, which proved effective over the years in preparing efficient teachers.

Allen and Ryan (1968) described microteaching as "a scaled down teaching encounter, scaled down in terms of class size, lesson length and teaching complexity".

Allen and Eve (1968) explained microteaching as "a system of controlled practice that makes it possible to concentrate on specific teaching skills and to practice teaching under controlled conditions".

Buch (1968) defined that "microteaching is a teacher education technique which allows teachers to apply well defined teaching skills to carefully prepared lessons in a planned series of five to ten minute encounters with a small group of real students often with an opportunity to observe the results on videotape".

Young (1969) described that "microteaching is a safe practice ground for student teachers, class room management problem can be minimised and focussed upon separately as a component skill".

McAleese and Unwin (1971) suggested that "the term microteaching is most often applied to the use of closed circuit television to give immediate feedback of a student teacher's performance in a simplified environment".

From the above definitions we can say, in essence, that microteaching is a scaled down teaching encounter, and also a system of controlled practice that makes it possible to concentrate on specific teaching skills, classroom management and the use of closed circuit television to give immediate feedback.

Concept of Microteaching

Teaching constitutes a number of verbal and non-verbal acts. A set of related behaviours or teaching acts aiming at specific objectives to facilitate student learning can be defined, observed, measured and controlled by means of practice. Microteaching encounters on specific teaching behaviour and provides opportunity for practice teaching under controlled conditions (Sampath and others, 1986).

Basically, microteaching is a 'scaled-down teaching encounter' in which a teacher teaches a small unit to a group of 5 to 10 pupils for a small period of 5 to 10 minutes. The complex act of teaching is broken down to simple components, making the task more manageable. Only one skill is attempted and practiced during a microteaching lesson. How to teach is considered more important, than what to teach. Such a situation offers a helpful setting for our experienced or inexperienced teacher to acquire new teaching skills and to refine old ones. It is also highly individualised training programme and it is to develop certain teaching skills are not the development of pupils abilities. Microteaching is a new design for teacher education which provides student teachers with information about their performance immediately after completion of their lesson.

The standard use of the term 'microteaching' involves a programme of following type:

1. A particular skill is defined to student teacher in terms of teaching behaviours and the objectives with such behaviours are aimed at achieving;
2. Videotapes or films on specific skills are shown or written material provided to demonstrate the teacher's use of particular skill in microteaching or in normal classroom teaching situation;
3. The student teacher plans a short lesson in which he can use the skills;
4. The student teacher teaches the lesson to a small group of pupils which is videotaped or audio-taped or observed by supervisor and/or peer(s);
5. Feedback is provided to the student teacher by video-tape or audio-tape, who observes and analyses his lesson with the help of supervisor. The supervisor attempts to make reinforcing comments about instances of effective use of the skill and draws the student teacher's attention to other situations where the skill could have been exercised;

6. In the light of feedback and supervisor's comments, the student teacher re-plans the lesson in order to use the skill more effectively;
7. The revised lesson is re-taught to different but comparable group of pupils;
8. Feedback is again provided (re-feedback) on the re-teach lesson which is analysed with the help of supervisor;
9. The 'teach-reteach' cycle (4 to 7 steps) may be repeated till adequate level of skill acquisition takes place.

Microteaching Skills

The concept underlying microteaching assumes that teaching is a complex process and it consists of several purposeful skills. A skill can be defined 'as a set of teacher behaviour which is specifically effective in bringing about desired changes in pupils. The basic contention is that, more the number of skills in which a person is trained, the more efficient he or she will be as a teacher.

The Australian Advisory Committee on Research and Development in Education have analysed teaching into the skills. Allen and Ryan of the Stanford University have suggested 14 skills that are representative of general teaching skills. Based on the lists of teaching skills developed at Stanford University, the Baroda General Teaching Competence Scale (BGTC) has been evolved with emphasis on the development of 21 skills. B.K. Passi (1976) has described 13 skills in detail with the components of each in his book "Becoming Better Teacher". The important microteaching skills are:

- Skill of writing instructional objectives
- Skill of introducing a lesson
- Skill of fluency in questioning
- Skill of probing questioning
- Skill of explaining
- Skill of illustrating with examples
- Skill of stimulus variations
- Skill of silence and non-verbal cues
- Skill of reinforcement

- Skill of increasing pupil participations
- Skill of using black board
- Skill of achieving closure
- Skill of recognizing attending behaviour

All these skills have been classified as pre-instructional presentation, closing, evaluation and managerial skills.

Considering the role and importance of microteaching in the teacher education programme, this study has been undertaken to study the attitude of prospective teachers towards microteaching.

STATEMENT OF THE PROBLEM

A Study of Attitude of Prospective Teachers towards Microteaching.

NEED OF THE STUDY

Teaching means creating an environment for learning. There are several components of this environment, viz., the learner, the learning situation, the teacher and the interaction that goes in between learners and teacher. Teaching technique used in a particular teaching learning environment depends on many factors including objectives, teaching methods, ability of students, and personality and experience of teacher. It helps the teacher to acquire mastery over teaching. Teaching technique not only helps in better understanding of teaching on the part of the teachers but also improves training effectiveness through simplifying the training task to be learned. At the same time, it ensures progressive mastery of the complex teaching skills. So, the main task of the teacher is to prepare and use the materials that are organised and presented in such a way so as to increase the teaching efficiencies of student teachers to maximise teaching process.

Therefore, research in the area of teaching and teaching behaviour has received some attention. During the last few decades many doctoral studies were conducted in the area of teaching in India. Most of them are found in the area of teaching techniques. Studies conducted in the area of teaching are found to be dominated by a few popular teaching techniques.

There is a need to select the techniques of teaching which would be applicable, functional and workable in Indian situation. These are to be acceptable to teacher educators and teachers. Thus, there is a need to study the feasibility of the techniques of teaching in terms of the attitude of student teachers towards microteaching.

Microteaching, as a technique of teaching, is selected for training because it is easy to handle, has wide applicability across subjects and has acceptability by teachers due to its analytical approach to teaching and more classroom applicability.

With the training of techniques, there is paramount importance to develop an effective strategy of training in techniques of teaching suitable for Indian conditions and acceptable to teacher educators for providing training to new entrants. Hence, it is necessary to study, at the outset, the attitude of student teachers towards microteaching and its feasibility before adopting it in the training programmes with a view to modifying, improving and strengthening such programmes.

SCOPE OF THE STUDY

The present study is confirmed to Guntur district of Andhra Pradesh. The sample selected for the study was prospective teachers who were studying in the College of Education and the sample size chosen for the present study is 200 prospective teachers.

The variables chosen for the study were gender (male and female), locality (rural and urban), teaching methodology (arts and science), educational qualification (P.G. and degree), and medium of instruction (Telugu medium and English medium).

The other factors that are related to the present study are achievement, concept level, intelligence, thinking pattern, etc., are not taken into consideration because of the constraints such as money, time, human resources, etc.

OBJECTIVES OF THE STUDY

The following objectives are framed for the present study:

1. To find out the attitude of student teachers towards microteaching;

2. To find out the difference between the attitude of male and female student teachers towards microteaching;
3. To find out the difference between the attitude graduate and postgraduate student teachers towards microteaching;
4. To find out the difference between the attitude of science and arts student teachers towards microteaching;
5. To find out the difference between the attitude of Telugu medium and English medium student teachers towards microteaching.

EDUCATIONAL IMPLICATIONS OF THE STUDY

Most of the student teachers may have favourable attitude towards microteaching, which may indicate that microteaching has direct relevance to the teacher education programme as a powerful supplement to the existing teacher education programme. Therefore, the empirical evidence may urge the teachers and administrators to adopt microteaching as an effective teaching technique in the field of teacher education.

2

Review of Related Literature

Review of related literature provides theories, ideas, and explanations of a new problem. It suggests methods, procedures, sources of data and statistical techniques appropriate to the solution of the problem. It helps to sharpen and define understanding of existing knowledge of the problem area and provides a background for the research project. It is also helps the researcher not only in providing information available in the field of research but in suggesting the methods to be adopted, avoiding the mistakes done by others and in locating misconceptions in the earlier discoveries by others.

Review of literature, thus, helps the researcher in the identification of the problem, in the selection of methods, tools and data analysis techniques and also in guarding against the likely pit-falls in the process of research. The researcher stands to gain from the experiences of other early researches in the field and gets guidance from them. He/she collects all possible solutions to the problem under study, all possible ways of interpreting the phenomenon being studied or all possible ways of understanding the true nature of the knowledge being discovered. From all the possibilities so collected, the researcher will select a feasible one to try out.

Research takes the advantage of the knowledge which has accumulated in the past as a result of constant human endeavours. Any worthwhile research in any field of knowledge requires an adequate familiarity with the work which has been done already in the same area. A summary of the writings of recognised authorities and of previous research provides sufficient evidence that the research is familiar with what is already known and what is still unknown. Since the effective research is based upon previous knowledge, this step helps to eliminate the duplication of what has been already done besides helping in fixation of useful objectives, formation of appropriate hypotheses, drawing of meaningful conclusions, and making commendable suggestions. (Bhaskara Rao, D., 1989)

Citing studies that show substantial agreement and those that seem to present conflicting conclusions help to sharpen and define understanding of existing knowledge in the problem area, provide a background for the research project and make the reader aware of the status of the issue. Parading a long list of annotated studies relating to the problem is ineffective and inappropriate, only those studies that are plainly relevant, competently executed and clearly reported should be included in the review of related literature (Bhaskara Rao, D. 1997)

A brief review of the previous investigations pertaining to the present study is very essential as it gives the present investigator an understanding of the previous works that have been done and also enables the investigator to know the means of getting to the frontier in the field of study. Unless it is learnt what others have done and what still remains to be done, the present investigator cannot develop a research project that would contribute to furthering knowledge in the field.

The research for related literature is a time consuming process. Even then, it is necessary for a good research. Hence, this chapter is meant for the study and citation of theoretical perspectives and research studies related to the present study on "A Study of Attitude of Prospective Teachers Towards Microteaching".

THEORETICAL PERSPECTIVES

Here the theoretical perspectives related to microteaching are clearly explained and discussed.

Microteaching is a teaching laboratory in which small groups of five or six faculty and two facilitators explore the process of teaching and learning by alternately teaching and responding as learners. We learn from feedback on our own teaching, from being student while others teach, and from the conversations about these experiences. The basic premise of microteaching is that there are many different ways to be an effective teacher and that we can expand our effectiveness by observing other teaching styles and strategies and by discussing shared issues of teaching and learning, no matter our discipline, unique style, or years of experience. In fact, we try to make sure that each small group has a wide diversity. In a sense, microteaching is a way of getting a mini-liberal arts education. (ACS Summer Teaching Workshop, USA)

The process of microteaching is as follows each person teaches a seven-to-eight-minute segment of a class; others respond as students. You might think about bringing a visual (a slide, overhead transparency, painting, cartoon, chart, graph, etc.) or a short text (a half-page or less) that has power to evoke or illustrate a key concept. If you are using a handout, bring eight copies. In short though, be yourself. Do whatever it is you normally do in your classroom and treat the other participants as your regular students. Think of seven-minute segment as a 'slice' of a whole class; it will not be a complete class, nor will it be a condensed version of a complete class. Ideally, the slice should happen as if a group of people walked into your regular class for seven minutes. We hope that you will experiment with your teaching during the workshop—at least on the final day, but perhaps in each session. Those not presenting will participate as students, and when the teaching segment is finished, they will offer constructive feedback. We will videotape both the teaching segment and the feedback session. This may at first seem a little outward, but participants quickly become accustomed to the camera usually, a seven-minute slice of teaching easily generates thirty minutes or so of discussion. Time goes very quickly, as you will see in your first segment. Facilitators will enforce time limits strictly, so that everyone has an equal chance to teach and to receive feedback. (ACS Summer Teaching Workshop)

Microteaching is a training concept that has been applied at the pre-service and in-service stages in professional development of teachers. Microteaching provides teachers with a practice setting for instruction in which the normal complexities of classroom are reduced. In it the teacher receives a great deal of feedback of his performance. (R.N. Sharma)

Meaning of Microteaching

Microteaching is so called since it is analogous to putting the teacher under a microscope so to say while he is teaching so that all faults in teaching methodology are brought into perspective for the observers to give a constructive feedback. It eliminates some of the complexities of learning to teach in the classroom situation such as the pressure of the length of lecture, the scope and the content of the matter to be conveyed, the need to teach for a relatively long duration of time (usually an hour) and the need to face large numbers of students, some of whom are hostile temperamentally.

Microteaching also provides skilled supervision with an opportunity to get a constructive feedback. To go back to the analogy of the swimmer, while classroom teaching is like learning to swim at the deeper end of the pool, microteaching is an opportunity to practice at the shallower and less risky side. (N. Anantakrishnan)

Microteaching is a teaching method where by the teacher reviews a videotape of the lesson after each session, in order to conduct a post-mortem. Teachers find out what has worked, which aspects have fallen short, and what needs to be done to enhance their teaching technique. Invented in the mid 1960s at Stanford University by Dwight Allen, microteaching has been used with success for several decades now, as a way to help teachers acquire and home new skills.

In the original process, a teacher will be asked to prepare a short lesson (usually 20 minutes) for a small group of learners who may not be his/her own students. This will be videotaped. After the lesson, the teacher, teaching colleagues, a master teacher and the students together view the videotape and comment on what they saw happening, referencing the teacher's learning objectives. Seeing the video and getting comments from colleagues and students provided, teachers with an often intense 'under the microscope' view of their teaching. (Microteaching - Wikipedia)

Microteaching is a scaled-down, simulated teaching encounter designed for the training of both pre-serve and in-service teachers. It has been used worldwide since its invention at Stanford University in 1960s by Dwight W. Allen, Robert Bush, and Kim Romney. Its purpose is to provide teachers with the opportunity for the safe practice of an enlarged cluster of teaching skills while learning how to develop simple and single concept lesson in any teaching subject. Microteaching helps teachers improve both content and methods of teaching and develop specific teaching skills such as questioning, the use of examples and simple artifacts to make lessons more interesting, effective reinforcement techniques, and introducing and closing lessons effectively. Immediate, focussed feedback and encouragement, combined with the opportunity to practice the suggested improvements in the same training sessions, are the foundations of the microteaching protocol. (Dwight W. Allen and Weiping Wang)

Microteaching is a training procedure aiming at simplifying the complexities of regular teaching process. In a microteaching procedure, the trainee is engaged in a scaled down teaching situation. It is scaled down in terms of class size, since the trainee is teaching a small group of four to six pupils. The lesson is scaled down in length of class time and is reduced to five or ten minutes. It is also scaled down in terms of teaching tasks. (J.C. Aggarwal)

Microteaching is a training technique which is called 'micro' since a teacher trainee practices with a small group of 5 to 10 pupils for a short duration of 5 to 10 minutes on a selected concept of lesson and concentrates on a single skill which is magnified. Teaching skills for student teachers focus on participant's observation skills, model teaching, discipline techniques, and content teaching. Microteaching is not a substitute, but a supplement to the teacher education programme. (A. Ram Babu, 2007)

Allen, D.W. (1966) says that microteaching is a scaled down teaching encounter in class size and class time. Allen, D.W. and Eve, A.W. (1968) explain that microteaching is a system of controlled practice that makes it possible to concentrate on specified teaching behaviour and to practice teaching under controlled conditions.

Buch, R.N. (1968) defines microteaching as a teacher education technique which allows teachers to apply clearly defined teaching skills to carefully prepared lesson in a planned series of five to ten minutes encounter with a small group of real students, often with an opportunity to observe the result on video-tape.

Clift, J.C. and Others (1976) state that microteaching is a teacher training programme which reduces the teaching situation to a simpler and more controlled encounter achieved by limiting the practice teaching to a specific skill and reducing time and class size.

Encyclopaedia of Education (Deighton, L.C., 1971) defines that microteaching is a real, constructed, scaled down teaching encounter which is used for teacher training, curriculum development and research. To Passi, B.K. and Lalita, M.S. (1976), microteaching is a training technique which requires student teachers to teach a single concept using specified teaching skill to a small number of pupils in a short duration of time.

Jangira, N.K. and Singh, Ajit (1982) suggest that microteaching is a scaled down teaching encounter or miniature classroom teaching. Singh, L.C. (1977) defined microteaching as a scaled down teaching encounter in which a teacher teaches a small unit to a group of five pupils for a small period of 5 to 20 minutes. Such a situation offers a helpful setting for an experienced or inexperienced teacher to acquire new teaching skills and to refine old ones.

La Dve (1970) states that microteaching is an opportunity to gain classroom capabilities and expertise before a student teacher start entering the teaching situation. Flanders, Ned. A. (1970) states that microteaching programme is organised to expose the trainees to an organised curriculum of miniature teaching encounters, moving from the less complex to the more complex.

M.C. Knight (1971) also stated that microteaching is a scaled down teaching encounter designed to develop new skills and refine old ones. McAlesse and Unwin (1971) suggest that microteaching is a scaled down teaching encounter in terms of time, class, size, lesson, length and teaching complexities. Jangira, N.K. and Singh, Ajith (1982) also say that microteaching is a scaled down teaching encounter or miniature classroom teaching.

Miltza (1978) states that microteaching is an opportunity to present something and then analyse the outcome; the two crucial elements are the ability to see oneself in action and analyse what was done.

Jangira (1980) opinion that microteaching is a training setting for the student teachers where complexities of normal classroom teaching are reduced by practising a particular teaching skill, for five to ten minutes on five to ten pupils using single concept.

Kumar (1996) feels that microteaching is a technique of training in which one learns the skills of teaching through a scaled down process of teaching learning. Singh (1979) is of the opinion that microteaching is a design for teacher training, which provides trainees with information about their performance immediately after completion of their class.

Turney, et al (1976) defined microteaching as teaching in miniature where it is scaled down in terms of class, size and task; the focus is on a specific skill.

Why Microteaching

Various authors explained the need or importance of microteaching in different ways.

Ryburn says that teaching is a relationship which helps to child to develop his powers. There are different methods or techniques to develop the powers of the child to modify teacher's behaviour, viz., microteaching, simulated teaching, interaction analysis and programmed instruction. Of all these methods, microteaching provides training of teaching skills to the student teacher under the controlled conditions. Simulated teaching is a role-play technique, which includes microteaching technique in artificial situations instead of real situations. Interaction analysis is an observation, which takes place between the teacher and the pupils to identify the complete behaviour of the teacher in his entire teaching process instead of observation of one skill. Programmed instruction is a self-study package, which does not observe the teaching skills. But, microteaching is a technique, which develops the particular skills in real situations to facilitate perfection in teaching. (A. Ram Babu).

Teaching is a complex task involving a large number of teacher activities. Both overt and covert teacher behaviours come into play. Overt behaviours are those which are 'open to view', i.e., observable, measurable and recordable. Covert behaviours refer to those which bring about a change in opinions and beliefs. Often, covert behaviours lead to overt behaviours. There may be as many as 500 to 700 such micro-overt behaviours per minute of a teacher in a classroom. In a 50-minute class, therefore, one expects 25000 to 35000 micro-behaviours. It is the grouping of such desirable micro-behaviours which constitute teaching skills. For example, the skill of asking questions consists of micro-behaviours covering standing still, thinking, framing a question, facing the students, listening, looking around for a response, recalling the names of students, calling students by names, pausing to think, etc. Different teaching skills are not exclusive to each other. A larger number of such micro-behaviours may be common to them. There being no way to measure as large as 30,000 micro-behaviours. It is better to identify some observable skills and then devise means to quantify them. Microteaching is all about demonstrating, quantifying and improving such teaching skills. (K. L. Kumar)

Derek Bok Center for Teaching and Learning, Harvard University, defines "Microteaching is organised practice teaching. The goal is to give instructors confidence, support, and feedback by letting them try out among friends and colleagues a short slice of what they plan to do with their students. Ideally, microteaching sessions take place before the first day of class, and are videotaped for review individually with an experienced teaching consultant. Microteaching is a quick, efficient, proven, and fun way to help teachers get off to a strong start".

How to Micro-teach?

As many as six teachers from the same or similar courses can participate in a single microteaching session. Course heads, a few experienced instructors, and staff members are usually invited to serve as facilitators. While one person takes his or her turn as teacher, everyone else plays the roles of students. It is the job of these pretend pupils to ask and answer questions realistically. It is the job of the pretend teacher to involve his or her class actively in this way.

Such a scenario typically runs for five to ten minutes. When finished, the person conducting the class has a moment or two to react to his or her own teaching. Then everyone else joins in to discuss what they saw that they especially liked. Finally, the group may mention just a few things that the practice teacher might try doing differently in the future.

What to Prepare?

Most course heads provide micro-teachers with scenarios to prepare in advance. If not, think of a few minutes of material that you especially would like to make sure your students understand by the end of your next class. As, always, you should not only plan out how to treat the subject matter, but also give some thought to how you are going to present yourself, manage the class, and involve the students. There are, of course, many different ways of teaching a given lesson well. That is why participants find that, along with what they learn from their own experience practice teaching, they can also pick up many helpful ideas from observing fellow micro-teachers.

The New Micro-teaching Simplified

Dwight W. Allen and Weiping Wang explain "The New Microteaching" as follows:

In the late 1980s and 1990s microteaching was reinvigorated with a completely new format developed in Southern Africa and later in China. Because of the lack of available technology in developing countries, microteaching's format had to be made less technology dependent in order to be useful. Early modifications were made in Malawi, but it was in Namibia and China where microteaching was completely transformed.

Twenty-first-century microteaching increases training effectiveness using in even more scaled-down teaching simulation environment. The new microteaching format was primarily shaped as a response to in-service teacher education needs in Namibia, where the vast majority of teachers were uncertified and there were few resources with which to train them. In China, it became part of a national effort to modernise teaching practice. Three important new concepts were incorporated:

1. *Self-study groups:* Teachers rotate between the roles of teacher and student, building on earlier versions of 'peer microteaching'. Self-study groups of four or five teachers have become the norm;

2. *The 2 + 2 evaluation protocol:* In earlier versions of microteaching, rather elaborate observation protocols had been developed to evaluate performance for each teaching skill. In the new microteaching, each new skill is introduced to trainees in varied combinations of face-to-face training sessions, multimedia presentations, and printed materials. These training materials give cued behaviours to watch for and comment on in the accompanying microteaching lesson. After a microteaching lesson is taught, each of the teachers playing a student role provides peer evaluation of the teaching episode using the 2 + 2 protocol — 'two compliments and two suggestions'. Compliments and suggestions are focussed on the specific skill being emphasised, but may relate to other aspects of the lesson as well;

3. *Peer Supervision:* Originally, the microteaching protocol required the presence of a trained supervisor during each lesson. However, with minimal training the compliments and suggestions of peers can become powerful training forces. Trainees feel empowered by the practice of encouraging them to evaluate the compliments and suggestions they receive from their peers (and supervisors, when present), allowing them the discretion to accept or reject any or all suggestions. On average, about two-thirds of the suggestions are considered worthwhile and suggestions from peers and trained supervisors are about equally valued.

The new and simplified format — widely used in the United States as well as abroad in the early twenty-first century — also makes it easier to incorporate the full, recommended protocol of teaching and re-teaching each lesson for each student. The microteaching experience goes well beyond the formal, narrow training agenda. The Gestalt experience of planning and executing a brief lesson that is closely monitored and scrutinised and the offering and receipt of feedback from respected peers is an integral part of the experience. In the present format, students often have three or four complete microteaching cycles in a single course. More cycles tend not to be well received by students, as the training format seems to break down after about four cycles. Some in-service training programmes have received enthusiastic reception from students for periodic microteaching sessions (one session each term or semester) over an extended period of time.

The flexibility of allowing each microteaching self-study group to make its own schedule, find its own location, and organise its own training and feedback procedures becomes an important part of the training experience. This leads to substantial savings of resources and allows the number of scheduled sessions to be determined by academic merit, not resource limitations.

Variants of Microteaching

Over the years, many microteaching clinics have made modifications in the basic training protocol that detract from the effectiveness of microteaching training, but are thought necessary, given the constraint of resources. Some of the most frequent of these modifications includes greatly increasing the size of the microteaching class. Sometimes, an entire class of twenty to thirty-five students is used as the microteaching class. This is necessary for scheduling reasons and because of the lack of facilities and staff for multiple, simultaneous sessions. This adaptation requires students to be passive learners for large numbers of lessons as each trainee has a turn to teach. The number of students in each class means that students teach very infrequently, often only once, and usually have no opportunity to reteach.

Another adaptation is the use of longer lessons, often fifteen or twenty minutes in length, because it is difficult to fit some lesson concepts into a five-minute lesson. This difficulty results from a lack of understanding of a single lesson element. A typical lesson will combine multiple concepts within the same topic, yet teachers often are not trained to break down their lessons into individual concepts. Identifying single concepts and planning a single concept lesson is itself an important skill. Microteaching is well suited to help teachers identify single concepts and learn how to create learning modules from which longer lessons can easily be constructed. Longer lessons in microteaching greatly increase the complexity and duration of training sessions, reduce the number of sessions possible for each individual trainee (unless the length of training is increased), and tend to cause the training sessions to lose focus. Microteaching research at Stanford University repeatedly showed that a five minute lesson is sufficient for the practice of many useful teaching skills in all subject areas.

The development of elaborate microteaching facilities, sometimes with permanent installation of multiple cameras, one-way glass partitions, and even audio capability at each student desk, has been another development. Though, very well intentioned, such clinic facilities have not proven cost-effective for the widespread use of microteaching. These facilities are even more personnel intensive. Often, special technicians are assigned along with a supervisor/proctor. These facilities would be more effective if the videotaping capacity was entrusted to students, thereby reducing the cost. The ideal would be for one out of every three or four sessions to be videotaped with a simple, one-camera setup with the opportunity to view the lesson immediately. When videotaping is not available and lessons are not taped, the training results have been found to be quite acceptable, though not optimal.

Microteaching Models of Teaching Skills

Microteaching can be an effective tool for the development of teacher training materials. When training protocols are being created to demonstrate new teaching skills, microteaching sessions can be developed and taped giving instances and non-instances of the skill. Asking trainees to view these tapes together is an effective way to highlight and demonstrate the essential aspects of the skill being taught.

Microteaching Courses

Microteaching has been developed as a course in many teacher-training institutions around the world. It readily combines theory with practice. When one considers that teacher trainees in many training programmes do their practice teaching under inadequate supervision with no student feedback, the relative merits and economy of microteaching become more and more apparent.

Microteaching offers the advantages of both a controlled laboratory environment and realistic practical experience. It is hardly a substitute for teaching practice, but it offers advantages such as close supervision, manageable objectives established according to individual trainee needs and progress, continuous feedback, an unprecedented opportunity for self-evaluation, immediate guidance in areas of demonstrated deficiency, and the opportunity to repeat a lesson whenever desired. When these advantages are combined with the economy of resources required to obtain them, microteaching becomes a valuable training method under many conditions throughout the world.

Materials for Microteaching

I. *Materials for Microteaching-1*

In your mentor teacher's classroom, you will introduce a unit of study, a week's lessons, or even a single lesson. You do not have to take the complete class period to do this. Plan this in conjunction with the teacher. You are to activate students' prior knowledge and tap the intrinsic motivation that they might have for the lesson/unit to follow. Turn in a plan to the teacher and to the instructor; this may be one plan turned in by two of you if you have been placed in the same setting. Each of you, however, must do a self-evaluation; questions are at the end of these materials.

(From materials developed by Tom Bacig, additions by Linda Miller Cleary)

Observation Guide for your initial visit to your mentor Teacher's Classroom

Observation allows you to develop invaluable skills which will pay off in teaching. Train yourself to be active in all parts of observation: watching and describing events in the classroom and recording your own feelings and responses to those events. During the classroom observation that you do in preparation for Microteaching #1, spend some time focusing and reflecting on the following issues. You will not be able to cover all these in one observation, but see how well you can do.

The Students

- How do groups communicate between one another? For example, do the students in the back or corners interact with the students in the front? Do the "popular" students interact with the other students?
- Who are the hand-raisers, non-hand-raisers?
- What is the students oral input like?
- How do students respond to the writing being done in the class?
- Do the students separate themselves by gender? Does gender have impact on the student's role in the classroom or success? How so?
- How do the weaker/less successful students behave? How do the capable students behave? Are provisions made for either group?

The Teacher

Remember this, teacher has given years to teaching and to students and deserves your respect. Nevertheless, you will be learning in your observations in this programme what kind of teacher you want to be. Be analytical, don't be judgmental, look for both the good as well as the things that you will do differently:

- How does the teacher begin the class? Pay attention to getting the students attention, his/her first gestures and words, how long it takes to get the lesson going.
- Does the teacher appear to interact with some students more than others? Think about gender, success level, social groups, etc.
- What does the teacher do when the student indicates non-comprehension-repeat, change language, explain differently, ask another student?
- How does the teacher respond to an incorrect or unexpected answer?

- Does the teacher have time to work with individual students?
- What happens when the bell rings?

The Instruction

- What kind of/how much reading do students do? Writing?
- What kind of literature and reading instruction occurs?
- How and when is the teacher's aim (rational, objectives) of the lesson communicated to the students?
- Can you discern a structure: e.g., introduction, presentation, demonstration, note-taking, individual/group work, discussion, summary, closure?
- How is the lesson brought to closure?
- How does the teacher evaluate whether the students have learned what was intended?

Set Induction: Getting Things Going in the Classroom

Introduction

The study of learning is basic to understanding of the teaching-learning process. Without knowledge of how and under what conditions a learner becomes involved in instructional activities, planning a learning environment is difficult.

The classroom environment, the specific teaching technique used, the place of the learning goal in the overall scheme of things—all contribute to the extent to which students become involved themselves in learning. In implementing plans for instruction, a critical role is that played by the introductory experiences a teacher uses to bring about the desired high level of involvement.

For the first microteaching you will first study techniques for set induction, then plan and try out specific procedures for getting things going in a classroom. Remember to use those things that motivate the student intrinsically to connect to and learn the concepts you want to teach:

1. Desire for feelings of competence;
2. Desire for feelings of self-determination;

3. Inclination towards imitation;
4. Responsiveness to feedback; and
5. Natural curiosity.

Things to Think About

How much does initial involvement in a learning task depend upon past success with similar tasks? anticipated rewards? natural interest? Effective interest and curiosity arousal by the teacher? clear understanding of the nature of the task? the need to know? self confidence? reasonable expectation of success? identified value to one's goals?

What classroom factors external to the student contribute to a positive set toward a learning task? How do these factors connect with the intrinsic motivations listed above?

Set Induction

Many teachers spend outrageously little time preparing their students for classroom activities. Often this preparation consists only of telling their students to read some story by the next class session or to watch some demonstration carefully. With such a limited introduction, could any teacher truly expect students to be attentive and eager to learn the material? The purpose of this microteaching is to stimulate you to think of better ways of preparing your students for learning.

Several psychological experiments have demonstrated the importance of set induction in learning. Research indicates that activities preceding a learning task influence the performance of the task. The research also indicates that the effectiveness of a set depends somewhat on the situation to which it is applied. Hence, teachers must find those kinds of sets most appropriate to their purposes and must modify these sets to fit the specific classroom situation.

In most cases, the initial instructional move of the teacher should be to establish a set. The set focusses students' attention on some familiar person, object, event, condition, or idea. The established set functions as a point of reference around which the students and the teacher communicate. The teacher uses this point of reference as a link between familiar and new or difficult material. Furthermore, an effective set encourages student interest and involvement in the main body of the lesson.

The establishment of a set usually occurs at the beginning of a class period, but it may occur during the session. Set induction is appropriate whenever the activity, the goal of the content of the lesson is changed so that a new or modified frame of reference is needed. Set induction is also used to build continuity from lesson to lesson and from unit to unit. Thus, a new set may be linked to an established set of to a series of sets.

All of us have experienced the influence of set induction on our responses to a situation. If we have been told that some person is a brilliant scientist, we respond differently than we would if we had been told he or she was a star athlete. What we learn during our conversation with this person will depend in part on what we have been told. Similarly, whatever information a teacher gives students about the degree of difficulty and format of a test will probably affect the way they study for it.

Suppose that a teacher wants the students to read chapter six in their textbooks as homework. Suppose chapter six is about the Constitutional Convention. What remarks or activities will produce the most learning for the next day? The teacher could say, "Now class, for tomorrow, I want all of you to read chapter six in the text." Such a weak set would normally produce a weak response. The next day the teacher might discover that half the class had not read the assignment, and that the other half, although claiming to have read it, was unable to discuss it in any depth.

The teacher might have said, "For tomorrow, I want you to read chapter six in the text and come to class prepared for a discussion." This set is an improvement. It gives the students more information about the instructional goal; they are to prepare for a discussion. But the students need a good deal more information before they will be able, or disposed, to prepare themselves for an interesting, stimulating discussion. Exactly what will be discussed? What points should they consider as they read? What should be the focus while they read? How should they use previously learned material? Should they study facts or principles? Should they compare? Should they contrast? Both? Neither?

The teacher could take a completely different approach to the Constitutional Convention of 1787. A different set, one more likely to motivate the students, might be something like the following:

Teacher: Suppose you were setting up a colony on a distant planet. Since this colony will be self-governing, the colonists have to draw up some kind of rules for governing themselves. For tonight I want each of you to pretend that you are a colonist on that planet, and that tomorrow you will begin discussions to draw up some sort of constitution. Think about who will do the ruling, how the ruler will be chosen, and what kind of rights each individual will be guaranteed. Also consider what the colony will do when its population expands to over a million people. Each one of you should answer these questions and be prepared to discuss them tomorrow.

After spending a subsequent class period discussing these and related questions, the teacher could assign appropriate reading and conduct discussions about the problems that confronted the Constitutional Convention in 1787. The teacher would have established a sufficient set, one that both stimulated the students and prepared them for the learning activity.

Sets are appropriate for almost any learning activity. For example, a set is appropriate:

- At the start of a unit;
- Before a discussion;
- Before a question-and-answer period;
- When assigning homework;
- Before hearing a panel discussion;
- Before student reports;
- When assigning student reports;
- Before a film or other media event;
- Before a discussion;
- Before a homework assignment based on a discussion that followed a filmstrip.

The most effective sets are those that catch the students' attention and interest them in the material. The following examples present learning activities or lesson material with ideas for appropriate sets:

1. *Lesson:* Tone in poetry/song.

   Set: Compare Bob Dylan with Rage Against the Machine

2. *Lesson:* Henry James' "Turn of the Screw"

   Set : Ask the students to decide if this is a ghost story or a story written by a neurotic who distorts reality.

3. *Lesson:* Shirley Jackson's "The Lottery"

   Set : Say, "Before we read "The Lottery," I want to finish giving grades. I've decided to fail three students. I have placed three slips in this hat that say "You fail" and thirty slips that say 'You pass.' Now we will pass the hat..."

4. Lesson: Student book reports.

   Set : Give examples of good book reports.

5. Lesson: Ordering and categorising behaviour.

   Set : Give the class CD cases. Ask them to sort the cases into four categories.

6. *Lesson:* Cultural differences.

   Set: Ask the students to imagine that they are Italians, and that you are an American walking down a street in Rome. Ask them if and how they could tell you were an American.

Student Presentations

Performing in Front of Others

(Prepared by Instructional Development Staff: R. Flagler, J. Hamlin)

One of the most stressful situations you are likely to be placed in is that of presenting material in front of a class. The process by which you present the material is equally as important as the content to be presented. Regardless of how well you have researched your topic, if the presentation is poorly prepared or unorganised the point will be lost. The audience will quickly lose interest.

Here are some tips and notes on how you can be most effective:

1. *Know your material:* Have your content well in hand. Most problems can be alleviated by being very well prepared. Be sure to do a complete job in your research and reading;
2. *Show interest in your topic:* Find something unique of special interest about the topic and most importantly, show your enthusiasm and interest. An enthusiastic presenter will get an enthusiastic audience;
3. *Know your audience:* Whom will you be presenting to? How involved with the topic is your audience? What level of sophistication does your audience have with the topic? Do you expect them to be asking questions? If so what kinds? What do you expect your audience to be doing during and after the presentation? You may need to tell them your expectations. How you present the material will foster questioning, comments or arguments;
4. *Outline your talk in advance:* The fewer notes you use the more natural your talk will be. Get a clear idea of the main points and supporting information, anecdotes, etc. Keep it simple and to the point. Be sure to utilise all the appropriate parts of a speech including introduction, body and conclusion;
5. *Make use of visual aids:* They are a good way to draw and maintain interest from your audience as well as highlight main points. Be sure they are appropriate and support your presentation. Check them out to be sure they work. When you are not referring to them, set them aside or cover them up;
6. *Practice your presentation:* Talk to yourself OUT LOUD going through all the motions and gestures you expect to use during your presentation. Make the practice as real as possible. Start practicing with your notes, you will quickly find you will no longer need them and your presentation will be more natural;
7. *Look sharp and expect butterflies:* Don't be fooled! Everyone is nervous to some degree, some people hide it better than others. Prepare yourself, this is an important event. Dress, eat, and sleep appropriately;

8. *Be yourself, Don't try to fake it:* You are who you are: smile, speak and gesture as naturally as possible. Remember the more you practice the more at ease you will become;

9. *Don't apologise:* Don't downgrade yourself by making excuses either at the beginning or the end of your presentation. Stand up. Give your talk with enthusiasm. Don't drag it out. Then, sit down and let others decide how well you did-unbiased by any apologies from you. Giving a good presentation requires skill. Above all, you must be well prepared and practiced. Be observant of others—watch what they do well and how you think they can improve.

Feedback

Giving Feedback—If you are placed with another student, you can give that student feedback to her/his lesson.

The following guidelines for effective feedback were adapted from Porter (1982):

1. Effective feedback describes situations or behaviour. Statements which evaluate or judge performance tend to make the receiver more defensive;

2. Feedback is most useful if provided soon after an observation has been made. Generally, feedback should be supplied immediately after a lesson or at the end of the day. In some instances the person being observed may need time to collect him/herself after an upsetting experience. The observer will need to assess when the receiver is ready to discuss the lesson;

3. Feedback is as specific and objective as possible. Script notes and audio and video tapes are excellent tool for providing feedback which is objective and specific;

4. Feedback is a two-way interaction and must consider the needs of both the sender and receiver. In providing feedback the sender must keep in mind the needs of the receiver. Feedback which only considers the sender's needs can be both frustrating and destructive to the receiver;

5. Feedback is most useful when it is directed at behaviour which the receiver can influence or change. Frustration and

resentment may occur when the receiver is informed of shortcomings which can not be controlled;

6. The sender should check to be sure that the receiver has understood the feedback. When feedback lacks clarity, misunderstandings may produce unintended results which are counterproductive;
7. Feedback may be provided by asking honest questions which are open-ended and encourage the receiver to analyse feelings, beliefs and behaviours. 'Trick' questions or questions which the observer already has an answer, may undermine the trusting and supportive relationship needed for effective analysis of classroom events;
8. Feedback needs to reaffirm the receiver's worth, competence and ability to achieve success.

Microteaching - 1 Self Evaluation to be done individually

Write a long paragraph for each

1. Describe how you came up with the idea you used for your set induction?
2. What beliefs about teaching entered into your planning of this set induction?
3. What did you notice in your viewing of the lesson on video about your use of non-verbal communication? about the effectiveness of your lesson? About areas in which you need to improve?
4. List two goals that you want to meet in your next microteaching (examples: I will get out from behind the podium and walk around. I will get each student to say something. I will get at least one discussion going between students instead of between myself and a student.)
5. Was there a difference between what you thought of your lesson before you saw the video and what you thought of it after your viewing?
6. What was the opening of your lesson like.

II. *Materials for Microteaching—2*

Short Discussion of a Poem or Short Story

Explanation

1. Microteaching — lead a short group discussion in your mentor teacher's classroom.
2. Lesson plans — submit a lesson plan to your instructor and to your mentor teacher.

Things to Think About

1. Have a 'clear opening' to the class.
2. What one or two concepts do you want students to come away with?
3. How will you or will you use the board or other visual aids?
4. What are the significant assumptions behind your rationale?
5. Do you have a variety of questions including literal, interpretive? Do you have both dense and shaded questions?
6. In what way might you let the students rehearse their responses to literature before the discussion?

Little Red Riding Hood

Level 1: Literal

1. Recall
   (a) Who made the cape and hood for Little Red Riding Hood (in our version it's only a red cap).
   (b) Where did Grandmother live?
   (c) Who came to the rescue of Little Red Riding Hood?
2. Convergence

Recopy and punctuate the following correctly:

Grandmother what big eyes you have the better to see you with my dear

Level II: Interpretation

1. *Categorising*

Judging from the story, which of the following adjectives would describe Little Red Riding Hood ?

a. thoughtful———

b. miserly———

c. aware———

d. rude———

e. suspicious———

f. critical———

g. naive———

h. kind———

i. concerned———

2. *Classifying*

Classify the following into three groups and give each group a heading:

Woods goodies jumped, running eyes looked, and walking killed picking.

3. *Comparing and Contrasting*

Compare and contrast the following:

Life Style Philosophy of Life

Wolf

Hunter

Make a statement comparing the Wolf and the Hunter

Make a statement contrasting the Wolf and the Hunter

4. *Association*

List all the things that come to mind when you think of "FAIRY TALE"

5. *Analysis*

Why did the author write the story?

a. to entertain?———

b. to teach behaviour?———

c. to clarify values?———

d. to teach values?———

e. to comment upon society?

Explain why:———

Give two examples of cause and effect in the story.

a. ————

b. ————

6. *Deductive Reasoning*

To which of the following would you relate this story?

a. Survival of the fittest———

b. Love of money (bread, food) is the root of all evil———

c. To the victor go the spoils———

d. If grandmother had been willing to work, she would not have needed the goodies———

e. Right is might———

Explain why:

7. *Inductive Reasoning*

Given the following facts, what generalization about life would you make?

a. Little Red Riding Hood's mother was concerned for the illness of the grandmother.

b. Little Red Riding Hood took time to take the basket to the grandmother.

c. The Wolf tried to subvert her mission.

d. Ignoring the implication of the Wolf's actions, she continued on her mission of mercy.

e. The Wolf outwitted the grandmother and almost outwitted Little Red Riding Hood.

Generalization———

8. *Critical Thinking*

Did the author present the Wolf as

a. A villain?———

b. A bright, alert, never-miss-an-opportunity business creature?———

How did you arrive at your choice of answer?

Level III: A New Understanding

i. Divergent

What other ways could Little Red Riding Hood has solved the problem of helping Grandmother after she met the Wolf? Give at least two ways.

ii. Syntheses

In today's society, what group of people might be represented by

a. The Grandmother?

b. The Wolf?

c. The Hunter?

d. The Mother?

e. Little Red Riding Hood?

iii. Concept Formation

In today's world, the cape might represent what concept?

iv. Creative Thinking

Writing the obituary notice for the Wolf from the standpoint of a reporter for the Daily St. Wolf's Chronicle.

Self-Evaluation for Microteaching — 2

1. Turn the sound off on the monitor and watch your non-verbal communication for a portion of your tape. Then imagine that you are a student in the class of this teacher. What non-verbal messages do you get? What makes this teacher approachable? What makes this teacher seem in control?

2. What goals for yourself did you meet in this microteaching?

3. Analyse your questioning? What kind of question elicited what kind of response? Use the white, shaded, dense designations or those described in "Little Red Riding Hood" above. If, as Collins and Seidman said, that students learn most when they make their own meaning of the content (text), how much meaning did your students make?

4. What different beliefs about teaching caused you to organise this lesson as you did? Did you revise any of your original plans based on your beliefs?

III. *Materials for Microteaching — 3*

Teaching Writing

(Group Work Option)

i. *Explanation*

1. *Microteaching* – In your mentor teacher's classroom, teach a writing concept. You may use group work for this microteaching (or in microteaching 4 or microteaching 6)

2. Lesson plans – turn in a plan for your lesson to your mentor teacher and to the course instructor (LMC).

3. Do an individual self-evaluation using the questions described below

ii. *Things to Think About*

1. Clear opening

2. Use of blackboard or other visual aids

3. Seating arrangement (depending on whether you use groups)

4. Teacher modelling of the concept you is teaching.

If you use the group work option, the following materials may be useful:

iii. *Student Checklist*

Cooperation

Name———

Group———

Date———

1. I contributed my ideas and information.
2. I asked others for their ideas and information.
3. I summarised all our ideas and information.
4. I shared my materials.
5. I asked for help when I needed it.
6. I helped the other members of my group leaın.
7. I made sure everyone in my group understood how to do the school work we were studying.
8. I helped keep the group studying.
9. I included everyone in our work.

Writing Prompt to get students to work together

iv. *Round Table Troubles*

King Arthur has a problem. The Knights of the Round Table are grousing about assignments. Lancelot insists that he only rescues maidens, due to his seniority and prowess as a knight. Galahad claims that he only seeks grails, and says it's beneath his dignity to bother with dragons. Sir Ulrich is willing to fight dragons but not slay monsters, and complains that Lancelot gets all the rescues. Sir Kay is willing to joust and help out with the monsters but he won't work overtime or on Saturdays. Lancelot is the best jouster, but says he is bored with it. Merlin insists he only works nights and refuses to answer his phone before midnight. Sir Seneschal and Sir Gawain are willing to do their duties, but complain that Lancelot gets all the prime cases, and that Sir Kay, Arthur's brother, gets to joust more often despite his second rate lance, while they have to do the dirty work. Sir Toby takes long lunches and insists that somebody has to stay home and guard the castle. Even the pages are upset. They claim that they are forced to do all the paperwork, write the reports (which the knights then sign) and then make all the copies and do the filing. They want more opportunities for advancement, pay commensurate with their actual work and some credit when they accompany a knight on an assignment.

King Arthur has orders for two maiden savings, three dragon slayings, two monsters to dispatch, three tourneys where the Round Table must be represented, and several requests from the Pope to seek out and return the Holy Grail. Formerly, he would dispatch whoever was available, but now the conflicting attitudes make this impossible.

Generally, rescuing maidens is soft duty with good benefits. Jousting is also preferred duty, with low risk and high expectation of gain, but opportunities must be balanced against maintaining the Round Table image. Grailing is high in prestige and considered a sacred duty, but since no one has ever found it, it tends to be a drag on a career, the seeker spending long years on the trail while his peers stay home and receive promotions. Monsters and dragons are usually dirty and unrewarding work, and carry a high risk (60% mortality) unless Merlin intervenes. Insurance agents for the Round Table insist that each assault on a dragon or monster be a separate policy, so that most of the loot goes for disability coverage.

King Arthur is tearing out his hair. To attempt to restore order to the Round Table, he has called in several groups of outside consultants to help sort out his administrative mess. The group with the best proposal will get the contract. Consider his problem and concoct a proposal which will solve his labour dispute and allow him to get on with saving the kingdom. Be prepared to present your solution to the class.

Microteaching

Elaboration (Erin Streblow)

(i) *Anticipatory Set*: Reveal a drawing of a plain stick figure on an overhead transparency.

(ii) *Objective*: To give students a listing impression through the use of drawing of the importance of elaboration in writing. Students will improve their elaboration skills through practice with their own writing.

(iii) *Reason its Importance:* Students need to recognise that sometimes just writing "the facts" isn't enough to create an engaging and effective piece of writing. Elaboration through detail, description and examples will make a work "come to life."

(iv) *Input and Modelling*: (5 min) I will reveal a second stick figure which I will start to elaborate by drawing hair, a face, clothes, etc. which will give it more character and interest. I will explain the analogy between bare bones writing and the plain stick figure in contrast to the much more interesting stick figure and elaborated writing.

(v) *Checking for Understanding*: (5 min) I will ask the students which adjectives describe the plain stick figure and those that describe the elaborated stick figure. Then ask them which type of writing they would rather read.

(vi) *Guided Practice*: (15 min) I will pass out paper and markers for everyone to draw two stick figures and elaborate one of them.

(vii) *Independent Practice*: (20 min) The students will take out a piece of writing they have been working on and will try to elaborate it by adding colour, texture, character, details, description etc.

(viii) *Closure:* (5 min) Students will share pictures/and writing with a neighbour and put pictures in writing folder as a reminder that elaboration is important in writing.

Self-Evaluation for Microteaching — 3

1. What was the pacing of your lesson like? Did you plan your time effectively for this ten minute session?
2. How were your voice, manner, and movement in this lesson?
3. What would this lesson do to improve student writing?
4. What do you think might be your strengths as a teacher? How will those strengths enhance your students learning?
5. What do you think might be a weakness for you in teaching? How can you compensate for that weakness?

IV. *Materials for Microteaching — 4*

Teaching a Language Concept Group Work Option.

Explanation

1. *Microteaching:* In your mentor teacher's classroom, teach a language concept. You may use groups for this microteaching (or in #6). Examples: grammar, language + power, dialects, vocabulary building, word choice, spelling, connotation/ denotation. Consider using the Concept Attainment Model or try your hand at some effective lecturing, along with other methods.
2. *Lesson plans:* (a) use the Madeline Hunter model of lesson plan for this lesson; (b) turn in one plan to your mentor teacher and one to the instructor.
3. Turn in an individual self-evaluation; use the questions below:

   Things to Think About

   1. What are my significant assumptions about language?
   2. Clear opening.
   3. How can the students connect with the concept you are teaching? How does that concept connect to their own worlds or the external world?
   4. Seating arrangement (if you are using groups)
   5. Use of board or other visual aids.

   Concept Attainment Model: Objective and Subjective Reporting

   (i) *Rationale:* The concept attainment model will provide students with an opportunity to discover a concept through an inquiry and discovery method which utilises classroom participation. The model allows the teacher to introduce a concept or unit by enabling the students to join in the introduction process. If students are made to recognise the difference between objective and subjective reporting, it will enable them to read between the lines in newspaper and magazine articles. Also, students will be able to formulate news articles and essays with a clearer idea of objectivity and subjectivity in mind.

(ii) *Objective:* The objective of the lesson is to have students discover the concept of objective reporting by examining news story leads. The students should be able to recognise characteristics familiar to all objective news stories. The student should be able to identify specific facts (who, what, when, where, why, how) while at the same time recognising that some kinds of reporting, while based on facts, have a subjective or bias slant.

(iii) *Method*: Students will be told that a new subject is being introduced through a concept attainment model approach to learning. Students will be told that they will be shown an example of the concept, followed by another example which, though similar, will not be an example of the concept. The examples will be written on cards and held up for the students to examine. The first example will be labelled a 'yes' example and placed in a 'yes' pile. The second example will be labelled a 'no' example and placed in a 'no' pile. Students will then be shown subsequent examples and be asked to guess whether or not the examples are 'yes' or 'no' examples. Examples should be left in clear view of the students, distinctly categorized 'yes' or 'no'. When students make an appropriate or inappropriate choice, they will be asked to state why they have made a particular choice. Students will be asked to identify like characteristics in both 'yes' and 'no' examples. Students should slowly be led to guess the concept.

(iv) *Evaluation:* Students will be able to identify examples as 'yes' or 'no' examples correctly. Students will be able to give reasons for their selection. Students will be able to identify characteristics familiar to objective news reporting. Students will be able to identify specific facts contained in the example leads presented, and in subsequent leads contained in actual newspapers. Students will be able to write leads objectively during a follow-up lesson.

Uses of the Lecture

(i) *To Convey Information:* A lecture can be used to convey information otherwise inaccessible to the students. For example, a specialist can offer information unavailable in textbooks.

(ii) *To Reinforce Written Work:* A lecture covering previously-learned material reinforces student learning through repetition. Use of this sort of lecture should be limited to emphasis of main points in the material.

(iii) *To Change the Pace:* Any teaching method, used exclusively, is boring. A teacher who relies only on classroom discussions might well profit by lecturing occasionally.

(iv) *To Synthesise Many Sources:* Lecturing is economical. A teacher is able to synthesise several sources, thus saving his students the trouble.

(v) *To Inform Students of Expected Results:* A lecturer can be a means of informing students of the expected results of a learning activity. If used in this way, it functions as an introduction to the activity by focussing the students' attention on the most important aspects of the material.

(vi) *To Convey Enthusiasm:* A lecture can convey to students the teacher's enthusiasm for a subject. An exciting lecture demonstrates the teacher's interest, which will stir the students also.

There is evidence that lectures are not appropriate when:

1. The instructional objective is other than the acquisition of information;
2. The instructional objective involves the application of skills;
3. The instructional objective involves the changing of attitudes or behaviour;
4. The information acquired is to be retained for a long time;
5. The material is complex or abstract;

6. Student participation in the learning activity is required;
7. The levels of intelligence and educational experience of the students are below average.

Effective Lecturing

Effective use of the lecture technique requires thoughtful consideration of the following factors:

(i) *Personality of the Lecturer*: A lecturer should be warm, friendly, and confident. He should speak clearly. He should have control of the language – syntax, word selection, enunciation, pronunciation, the use of meaningful figures, and so on. A teacher who lacks these characteristics should avoid using lecture;

(ii) *Consideration of the Audience*: Students must be sufficiently verbal to understand and respond to a lecture. For students who are not verbal to understand do not respond to a lecture. For students who are not verbally skilled, a lecture is rarely appropriate. Slow learners also find it difficult to respond to the concentrated material of a lecture. Other oral media, such as classroom discussion, are more effective for these students;

(iii) *Preparation of the Audience*: Students must be prepared to respond to the lecturing technique. The teacher should be sure that his students know how to listen for main ideas. Many students lack this skill;

(iv) *Planning and Organisation*: Effective lectures are planned lectures. The teacher's main points must be sharply defined, and the supporting material well-organised. "Tell them, what you're going to tell them, tell them, and tell them what you've told them" is an old but useful guideline. Summaries of main ideas, both at the beginning and at the end – and sometimes interspersed throughout the lecture – add to the students' retention. Summaries give the students an outline on which to hang details;

(v) *Vocabulary*: A teacher only communicates to students who can understand his language. For this reason, the teacher must carefully choose the vocabulary of his lecture;

(vi) *Repetition*: Repetition of the lecture's main ideas increases the chances that students will remember them. Repetition appears to be more effective than verbal emphasis, pauses, or gestures for stressing main points. But the teacher should avoid excessive repetition. Four or five repetitions of a single point will normally produce restlessness or boredom;

(vii) *Varied Stimuli*: Reading a lecture is usually less effective than speaking freely from a well-thought-out lecture plan. Reading tends to result in monotonic, dull delivery. Good lecturers vary voice pitch, loudness, intensity, and speed of delivery. Such variety of stimuli is more likely to hold attention. The speed of delivery should vary between 115 and 160 words per minute. Simple material should be delivered quickly; difficult material more slowly;

(viii) *Time Length*: Most lectures are too long. Even with a good lecturer and an interesting topic, the attention span of most audiences is short. For most school children, a lecture should be kept short; thirty minutes or less;

(ix) *Illustrative Devices*: Illustrative devices enhance a lecture and increase learning. But audio-visual materials must not be used for their own sake. To be appropriate, they must complement the lecture and enhance its effectiveness. Furthermore, students must be adequately prepared for their use.

Watch the film "Lecturing", if available Observe gestures, pacing, pitch and intensity of voice and rate of delivery of the speaker.

Prepare a short lecture to deliver. Be sure you can justify use of lecture for this particular instruction. Consider it as a possibility for Microteaching - 4.

If used, Microteaching - 4, evaluate as usual. Watch the videotape. Was your lecture well organised? Was the purpose understood? Did it logically progress? Check with your faculty supervisor and re-do if he thinks you need to.

Abstract ideas are easier to understand if related to concrete situations so teachers frequently give examples and illustrations.

Failure to provide examples or give illustrations may lead students to doubt the teachers' grasp of a concept.

There are two basic ways to use examples. In the deductive approach a teacher states an idea, gives clarifying examples to substantiate it and then asks students to give examples and relate these to the main idea. In the deductive approach, the teacher starts with examples. Students are asked to generalise from these to the desired conclusion. Failure to do so may result from poor skills in drawing references, or poor examples. Both of these are within the teacher's power to change.

Using the inductive approach, the teacher does not start with the idea. Instead, he starts the examples illustrating the idea. After studying the examples, the students try to generalise and make inferences. If the students fail to arrive at the main idea, then either they have not induced correctly, or the examples were misleading. In the former case, the teacher points out the fallacies in their inferences; the latter, the teacher find better examples. The teacher does not tell the students what the examples illustrate. Eventually, the students arrive at the correct generalisation themselves.

Analogies and metaphors are frequently used verbal illustrations. Comparisons that highlight the similarities between what is already known and what is being learned are analogies. These should be used carefully; they should not be stretched too far. Metaphors suggest resemblances beyond literal bounds, e.g., "His mind is like a sieve."

Two kinds of verbal illustration merit special consideration: the analogy and the metaphor. An analogy usually highlights similarities between a thing that is already understood and a thing that is not thus bridging the gap between the known and the unknown. For example, comparisons that indicate the similarities between a human heart and a pump, or a tank's armor and a crab's shell, are analogies. However, a teacher must be careful not to stretch analogies too far, as perfect ones are rare. Both of those given above, for example, are useful but imperfect. Imperfect analogies presented as perfect ones confuse students rather than enlighten them. The teacher should emphasise only those parts of the analogy that hold true, and he should point out imperfections.

A metaphor suggests a resemblance and is more vivid than a literal example. A metaphor is a word or phrase applied to something to which it is not literally applicable. The sentences, "His mind is a sieve," and "That horse is a bag of bones," each uses a metaphor. Metaphors and analogies, interspersed with literal examples, can enliven a teacher's explanation of a concept.

The following are guidelines for the effective use of examples:

1. Start with the simplest examples. Work from simple examples to complex ones. A basic principle of concept formation is that examples given to illustrate a concept confront the learner with a complex sorting task. Some of the information conveyed by the examples is relevant; some is not. If you begin with complex examples, the students may become confused by excess information and miss the point. Therefore, begin with simple examples and work up to complex ones, emphasising only the relevant aspects of each;

2. If examples are not within the range of the students' experience and knowledge, then they are useless as illustrations of a concept. How do you know that an example is appropriate for your students? This information is a function of your familiarity with your students' backgrounds. The more you know about your students, the more you will be able to select relevant examples;

3. After presenting some examples, sharpen your students' understanding by offering an irrelevant example—one that has no relation to the concept. In other words, once the students have acquired a basic understanding of the concept, present them with examples that do not illustrate the concept. This use of "non-examples" helps students discriminate between the concept you are teaching and other similar concepts. However, do not include a non-example too early in the presentation. Wait until the students are likely not to be confused by it;

4. Don't assume that the more examples you give the better the students will understand the concept. Unless the additional examples illustrate new aspects of the concept, or provide more information about it, they will add nothing to the students' understanding;

5. Remember that the point of using examples is to illustrate, clarify, or substantiate an idea. Therefore, you must relate the examples to the idea. Don't assume that students will automatically connect examples they are given with an idea. Either relates the examples to the idea yourself, or have the students do it;

6. One way to make sure that students have understood a concept is to ask them to give you additional examples of it. If their examples are good, they have probably grasped the concept. If their examples are faulty, they have probably misunderstood, and you can adjust the lesson accordingly.

Madeline Hunter's Mastery Teaching—Critical Attributes

(i) *Objectives*: Know, state, and teach your objectives

(ii) *Motivation*: Level of concern — Moderate level is essential for learning.

(iii) *Feeling tone*: Situation must be pleasant for the student.

(iv) *Success*: Must be possible for student to achieve.

(v) *Interest*: Must be useful to student's life.

(vi) *Knowledge of results*: Student must be aware of when the goal is accomplished.

(vii) *Anticipatory Set*: Getting students ready to learn.

(viii) *Input and Modelling:* Determine basic information and organization use of critical attributes. Present basic information in simplest and clearest form. Model information or process.

(ix) *Checking Students Understanding and Guiding Practice:* Monitor independent practice

(x) *Closure:* Summarise

Blank Form for Hunter Model

Anticipatory set:

Objective:

Reason it's important:

Input:

Modelling:

Checking for understanding :

Guided practice:

Independent practice:

Closure:

Student Examples

T. Williams, Madeline Hunter Model:

(i) *Objectives*: It is important for students to learn the difference between dialects and correctness. I want the students to see how they use language in school as opposed to other areas. I want them to examine some of the different words that they use and hear around the school and form a slang dictionary that can be used around the school;

(ii) *Motivation*: Hopefully this dictionary will be fun for the students to complete. I will explain that the teachers in the school sometimes have trouble with the words they use, and by completing the dictionary they will help the teachers with the slang around the school. I would like to publish the dictionary and sell it in the school for one dollar a-piece. The money that is raised would go towards new books for our classroom library. This would also be a positive influence for the students to see their names and work circulated around the school. The dictionary would be fun and easy for the students because it would be their own work with prior knowledge involved. I would like the students to base the dictionary on their own slang words and those of their peers. To accomplish this they can interview others in the school to complete the dictionary;

(iii) *Anticipatory Set*: I will give a brief introduction on slang and how it is used. I will give examples of slang and ask them to volunteer any of their own. After this, I will explain the purpose of the dictionary and how they should go about finishing it;

(iv) *Input and Modelling*: The students can use any slang that they can come up with, either through interviewing or brainstorming on their own. One rule that I will enforce is that no obscene language can be used in the dictionary. I will give them the chance to work in groups in order to brainstorm with each other. I will also stress the importance of interviewing so they get a bigger variety. I will model by giving them some of my own slang words that might be outdated or funny to them;

(v) *Checking Students' Understanding and Guided Practice:* I will circulate around the room when the students are in their groups to check for questions and help if they get stuck;

(vi) *Independent Practice*: The students will work on their own during the interviews and when they record the definitions of the slang words;

(vii) *Closure*: I will stress the importance of the dictionary to help the teachers better understand the students. I will also ask if there are any questions and ask some of my own in order to test their understanding.

Self-Evaluation for Microteaching-4 Teaching Language

1. Describe in one sentence the way that you used group work in one of your microteachings. From your observations of that tape, what benefits did those group experiences provide the class? How do you think you might have set up the group work or the assignment so that it would have been more productive for the groups?

2. What language concept did you teach to the class? Did you teach it inductively or deductively? In viewing the tape how would or did your method affect the grasp that your students had upon the concept when your lesson was complete?

3. Review your tape for Microteaching #1. How are you getting stronger as a teacher? What should your next steps be in becoming a fine teacher?

V. *Materials for Microteaching—5*

15 Minute Discussion

i. Explanation

(a) *Microteaching:* In 15 minutes, conduct a discussion on an issue, piece of literature, or theme that is being studied in your mentor teacher's classroom;

(b) *Lesson plans:* Turn in a copy to your mentor teacher and to your instructor.

Things to think about

1. Will you stand or sit?
2. Desk arrangement
3. Try to get students to discuss amongst themselves. Set students into arguing about reactions, idea, etc.
4. Try leading students to a theme you want them to discover and see how far it gets you.
5. Avoid "Do you think ?" statements, questions.
6. Try some open and closed questioning.
7. Try to have four dense questions and see what happens.
8. Try one question that you yourself don't know the answer to.
9. Check out "Little Red Riding Hood" again to find some Level 3 or Level 4 questions to try.
10. Try to divide the discussion in some way so that you and your partner have some autonomy in the experience, so that as an individual you can experiment and analyse the results.
11. Notice in the lesson plan below how the teacher has tried to rehearse the students for a discussion. Plan pre-reading, during reading, and/or post-reading activities to prepare for a good discussion.

An Example that uses Rehearsal to Generate Discussion

"The Stone Boy", By Gina Berriault, From Points of View. ed. J. Moffit and K. McElhony, 10th Grade English (USA).

Pre-reading Activity

(a) *Free Write*: In your journal, write for approximately 15 minutes about a personal experience in which you've received (or had to give) "bad news". If you were on the receiving end, how did you feel? If you were on the giving end, how did you act? Make two lists describing your feelings and actions. List at least five items for each. Example: When my brother's best friend was killed in a car accident, I had to help break the news to some of their friends.

(b) *Feelings Actions:* sad, upset, calm-made phone calls, helped family reach people.

Read "The Stone Boy"

Post-reading Activities: What might these be?

Self-Evaluation for Microteaching—5

Do a careful examination of the video of your lesson:

1. What kind of questions (dense, shaded, white, or the Little Red-Riding Hood question types) elicited what kind of response? Actually relisten to the tape, write down abbreviated forms of the questions you asked, identify the type of question, and evaluate the kind of response that it received. This analysis must be turned in with this self-evaluation. Take the time to do it. You will learn something from this analysis;
2. How much did the teacher talk vs. the students? Was the student talk focussed to other students or to the teacher?
3. How was the wait time? Was it productive or confusing?
4. What teacher behaviours were evident and how were they evident?

- Acceptance of students' feelings and ideas
- Encouragement

- Use of student ideas
- Giving directions
- Justifying authority
- Asking questions/stating opinions

VI. *Materials for Microteaching - 6*

Media/Drama/Technology Explanation

1. *Microteaching:* Teach a concept which relates to the media (TV, film, magazines, newspaper, etc.), or to technology, or to drama in your mentor teacher's classroom. You may use groups for this microteaching. Or teach a lesson in which you use media to further an objective.
2. *Lessons Plans:* Turn in a lesson plan to your mentor teacher and to your instructor in 5922. Fill out the individual self-evaluation below.

Things to think about

1. What are my significant assumptions about the role of this particular media in the lives of my students?
2. Room arrangement.
3. Do you know how the equipment works?
4. Clear opening set. This is crucial for audio-visual material or students are unsure of what to focus on.
5. How will you follow up (especially if you use a film or video)? A crucial time is the period immediately after a film when it may have to be rewound. Many a classroom disintegrates at this point. Wise planners plan an activity, discussion, written question, etc., (and ask a student to rewind the film).

Evaluation for Microteaching-6

1. Briefly describe the technology or media that you used in this microteaching and then tell the story (a brief version) of your lesson. Describe the knowledge and beliefs about teaching that influenced your plan, the events, and even your reflection on the event. Having re-viewed the

rationale for your lesson plan, how did the technology or media material further your rationale for teaching the lesson?

2. Openings and conclusions of lessons help orient the learner and then hammer home the lesson. How did you do in opening orientation and closing summaries?

3. Was the lesson or the technology in the lesson equally accessible to all?

4. Sometimes technology is a means to learning technology as opposed to a means to learning the language arts. Was your lesson more about technology or more about learning reading, writing, speaking, listening, thinking or literature? If your lesson was about media, were there aspects that were inaccessible to some students based on their prior experience?

Summative Evaluation of all the Microteachings (1 to 6)

1. From your observations of and discussion with the mentor teacher, what would you guess to be the classroom teacher's beliefs? Discuss how would your beliefs as a teacher change the way this classroom would go about learning if you were the only teacher in the class?

2. Tell me the story of your experience with teaching in a "real" school. Looking back on the term what happened? How did you experience it? Construct a narrative about how your teaching experience grew, succeeded, faltered, bloomed, etc., through the term.

3. Reread what you just wrote. Reflect on what happened, on your collective reactions or feelings about specific events, reasons for what happened, your evaluation of what happened, disparities between your plans or hopes and what happened, instances in which a different decision would have changed the course of what you were doing and why.

4. Think over what you need to work on during your student teaching. Talk about what strengths you have and how you might use those to work on what you still need to work on.

Characteristics of Microteaching

Following are some of the well known characteristics of microteaching defined by R.N. Sharma.

1. *Real Teaching*: Microteaching is real teaching. However, it focusses on developing teaching starts.
2. *Scaled down teaching*: The following outline is characteristic of scaled down teaching: (a) Scaling down the class size to five to ten pupils; (b) Scaling down the duration of period of five to ten minutes; (c) Scaling down the size of topic; and d) Scaling down the teaching skill.
3. *Individualised device:* It is a highly individualized training device.
4. *Providing feedback:* It provides the feedback for trainee's performance.
5. *Device for preparing teachers*: It is a device to prepare effective teachers.

J.C. Aggarwal summarised the characteristics and features of microteaching as:

1. Microteaching is relatively a new innovation in the field of teacher-education;
2. It is a training technique and not a teaching technique;
3. It is scaled down teaching:
   (a) which reduces the class size 5 to 10 pupils
   (b) which reduces the duration of period 5 to 10 minutes
   (c) which reduces the size of the topic
   (d) which reduces the teaching skill
4. It provides adequate feed-back;
5. Microteaching provides opportunity to select one skill at a time and practice it through its scaled down encounter and then take others in a similar way;
6. Microteaching is a highly individualised training technique;

7. Microteaching permits a high degree of control in practising a particular skill;
8. Use of videotape and closed circuit television makes observation very objective;
9. Microteaching is an analytic approach to training.

Assumptions of Microteaching

According to Allek and Ryan, microteaching is an idea at the core of which lie the following five essential propositions or assumptions:

1. *Real teaching*: Microteaching is real teaching. Although the teaching situation is constructed one in the sense that teachers and students work together in a practice situation, nevertheless, bonafied teaching does take place;
2. *Reduced Complexities:* Microteaching reduce the complexities of normal class-room teaching, class size, scope of content, and time;
3. *Focus on training:* Microteaching focuses on training for the accomplishment of specific tasks. Included among these tasks are the practices of technique of teaching, the mastery of certain curricular materials, and the demonstration of teaching methods;
4. *Increased control of practice:* Microteaching allows for the increased control of practice. The rituals of time and students are manipulated. In the practice setting of microteaching of a high degree of control may be built in to the training programme;
5. *Expanding Knowledge of Results:* Microteaching very much expands the normal knowledge of results for feedback dimension in teaching. The trainee engages in a critique of his maximum insight into his performance, several sources of feedback are put at his disposal. He analyses aspect of his own performance in the light of his goal with the guidance of supervisor or colleague. The trainee and the supervisor go over student response forms that are designed to elicit students' reactions to specific aspects of his teaching. If the supervision has video-tape available, he may use video-tape playback to show the teacher how he performs and how he may improve.

All this feedback can be immediately translated into practice where the trainee reteaches shortly after the critique conference.

Microteaching and Traditional Teaching

1. *Simple versus complex teaching*: While microteaching is simple traditional teaching is relatively complex and threatening.
2. *Specifications of objectives*: In microteaching the objectives are specified in behavioural terms, in traditional teaching there are specified in instructional terms.
3. *Providing Feedback*: While in microteaching important feedback is provided, in traditional teaching feedback is not provided
4. *Size of class:* While in microteaching the class is divided into small groups of five to ten pupils, in traditional teaching the class consists of fifty to hundred pupils
5. *Duration*: While in microteaching the duration is five to ten minutes, in traditional teaching the duration is forty to sixty minutes.
6. *Pattern of Classroom Interaction*: While in microteaching patterns of classroom interaction may be objectively studied, in traditional teaching the pattern of classroom interaction can not be objectively studied.
7. *Practicing skill*: While in microteaching the pupil-teacher practices only one skill selected for practice, in traditional teaching the pupil-teaching practices whole complex teaching behaviours.
8. *Role of supervisor*: While in microteaching the role of the supervisor is specific and well defined to improve teaching, in traditional teaching the role of supervisor is vague and not useful to improve teaching.
9. *Awareness*: In comparison of traditional teaching microteaching develops more awareness among student teachers with regard to professional training.
10. *Score*: In university examination microteaching results better score than their counterparts in conventional teaching.

Objectives of Microteaching in Colleges of Education

The following objectives of introducing microteaching in Colleges of Education have been enlisted by Duggal and Sharma:

- Initiating the teacher trainees to analyze and develop teacher behaviour under laboratory conditions;
- Landing the novice teachers gradually in the real classroom after gaining enough confidence;
- Imparting intensive training in the component skills of teaching to teacher trainees at pre-service level;
- Involving the academic potential of teacher trainees for providing feedback to the peers;
- Reducing the work load of teacher educators with the involvement of peer-supervisors;
- Reducing the burden upon practising schools while having practice of teaching skills under simulation conditions in Colleges of Education;
- Exploring the human resources to the maximum and making economic with regard to time, money and material.

A. Ram Babu (2007) defined the following objectives:

- To assimilate and learn new teaching skills under controlled conditions among the pupil teachers;
- To utilize the available material, money and time to the maximum;
- To provide required feedback;
- To develop confidence in teaching;
- To acquire mastery in a number of teaching skills;
- To simplify the teaching process;
- To attain perfection in teaching;
- To modify the teaching behaviours in the required manner;
- To reduce the complexity of teaching;
- To acquire new teaching skills and to refine old ones.

S. K. Murthy stated the following objectives:

- To lesson the complexities those exist in macro-classes and to give adequate practice teaching to students at shorter duration;
- To identify the deficiencies of trainees to give immediate feedback and help them to modify their teaching behaviours and to demonstrate the same in re-teaching a class in another micro-situation;
- To develop experimental teacher education programmes and to encourage research identifying new teaching skills;
- To improve teaching effectiveness through increased control of instructional practice and supervision.

Procedure of Microteaching

Microteaching procedure involves the following steps:

- *Defining the Skill*: To provide the knowledge and awareness of teaching. A particular skill is defined to trainees in terms of teaching behaviours;
- *Demonstrating the Skills:* The specific skills demonstrated by the experts are shown through video-tape or film to the teacher trainees;
- *Planning the Lesson:* With the help of his supervisors, the student teacher plans a short (micro) lesson in which he can practice a particular skill;
- *Teaching the Lesson:* The pupil-teacher teaches the lesson to a small group of pupils (i.e., 5 to 10 pupils). The teaching is observed by the supervisors or peers;
- *Discussion*: Teaching the lesson is followed by discussion to provide feedback (suggested improvements) to the trainee. The video-tape or audio-tape may be displayed to the trainee to observe his own teaching activities. The awareness of his own teaching performance provides the reinforcement to the pupil-teaching;
- *Re-planning*: The pupil-teacher replans the lesson in order to practice the small skill effectively in the light of the discussion and suggestions;

- *Re-teaching*: This replanned lesson is retaught to another small group of students of same class for the same duration to practice the small skill;
- *Re-discussion*: The re-teaching is now followed by discussion, suggestions and encouragements of the teaching performance. The feedback is again provided to the trainee;
- *Repeating the Cycle*: The cycle is repeated till the desired level of skills is achieved.

To conclude, in microteaching, the pupil-teacher tries to complete the 5 'Rs'. viz., Reciting, Reviewing, Responding, Refining and Redoing.

Microteaching cycle has been represented as follows:

Plan ——>Teach——>Discuss >and Feedback ——> Re-plan——>Re-teach <——Re-discuss and Re-feedback.

Clift and Others (1976) have suggested the following three phases of microteaching procedure:

1. ***Knowledge Acquisition Phase***

   It involves two major activities.

   (i) Observing demonstration skill.

   (ii) Analyzing and discussing demonstration.

2. ***Skill Acquisition Phase***

   Three activities are performed under this phase in the following sequence:

   (i) Prepare the micro-lesson

   (ii) Practice teaching skill

   (iii) Evaluate the performance

   The evaluation activity provides the basis to replan the lesson for reteaching the same topic to practice the same skill.

3. ***Transfer Phase***

   Now, after acquiring skills in the second phase, the pupil-teachers are given an opportunity to use the skill in normal classroom teaching situation.

S.K. Murthy defined the following steps in microteaching:

- Selection of the teaching skill to be practiced;
- Determination of micro-class, micro-content and micro-period;
- Preparation of microteaching plan;
- Undertaking of microteaching under supervision;
- Critique conference using video-playback and evaluation sheet;
- Re-planning;
- Re-teaching;
- Self-confirmation.

N. Ananthakrishan defined microteaching cycle as below:

The microteaching cycle starts with planning. In order to reduce the complexities involved in teaching, the student teacher is asked to plan a 'micro-lesson' i.e., a short lesson for 5 - 10 minutes which he will teach in front of a 'micro-class', i.e., a group consisting 3 - 4 students, a supervisor and peers, if necessary. There is scope for projection of model teaching skills, if required, to help the teacher prepare for his session. The student teacher is asked to teach concentrating one or few of the teaching skills enumerated earlier. His teaching is evaluated by the students, the peers and the supervisor using checklists to help him. Video recording can be done if facilities permit. At the end of 5 to 10 minutes sessions as planned, the teacher is given a feedback on the deficiencies noticed in his teaching methodology. Feedback can be aided by playing back the video recording. Using the feedback to help himself, the teacher is asked to replan his lesson keeping the comments in view and reteach immediately the same lesson to another group. Such repeated cycles of teaching, feedback and reteaching help the teacher to improve his teaching skills one at a time. Several such sequences can be planned at the departmental level. Colleagues and postgraduate students can act as peer evaluator for this purpose. It is important, however, that the cycle is used for helping the teacher and not as a tool for making a value judgment of his teaching capacity by his superiors.

Model of Microteaching

The CSUF Carnegie CASTL Programme Microteaching Workshop is a valuable opportunity to learn from colleagues outside of one's discipline teaching/learning techniques that can be adapted to one's own courses; to apply collegial constructive criticisms to improve one's own teaching/learning strategies; and, through assuming the students role, to sharpen one's insight into students' teaching/learning needs and expectations.

Microteaching was developed in the early and mid 1960s by Dwight Allen and his colleagues at the Stanford Teacher Education Programme. The Stanford model emphasised teach, review and reflect, re-teach approach, using actual school students as authentic audiences. The model has been adapted for college and university teaching where it has been used most often for graduate teaching assistants. It often offers a concentrated, focussed form of peer feedback and discussion.

A very similar model called Instructional Skill Workshop (ISW) was developed during the early 1970s by British Columbia's Education Ministry as a training support programme for all college and institute faculty in British Columbia and has now spread throughout Canada, the US and internationally. While there are significant differences between the two models, they both share some commonalities and were designed to enhance teaching and promote open discussion about teaching performance.

Indian Model of Microteaching

The Department of Teacher Education in the National Council of Educational Research and Training (NCERT) designed a project to study the effectiveness of microteaching in 1975 in collaboration with the Centre of Advanced Study in Education (CASE), Baroda. Research and training programmes for teacher educators were also initiated in collaboration with Department of Education, University of Indore in 1979. Instructional material on microteaching developed by Passi (1976), Singh (1976,1979) and Jangira (1978) was used for the training of teacher educators. Based on this research, NCERT developed the Indian Model of Microteaching. The silent features of this model are:

1. The mode of presenting the skill, i.e., modelling is done through written material, lectures, demonstrations and discussion and not through films, video or CCTV as in the case of advanced technology models of microteaching followed in the USA and the UK and other countries;
2. Live observers are used to observe teaching for providing feedback to the student teachers in the Indian Model, while CCTV is used in the developed countries. Peer supervisors are used along with college supervisors;
3. The microteaching laboratory can function with minimum of facilities according to the available space, material and equipment. Feedback sessions can be organised even in corridors or in open space;
4. The duration of the microteaching cycle is as under:

Teach	6 minutes
Feedback	6 minutes
Replan	12 minutes
Reteach	6 minutes
Refeedback	6 minutes
Total	36 minutes.

Principles Underlying in Microteaching

The following principles underlie the technique of microteaching:

1. *Principle of Practices*: 'Practice makes a man perfect' is of quoted proverb. If activity is repeated again and again, it is learnt effectively. Microteaching provides such practice in each small task of skill for the pupil-teacher to gain mastery over the practicing skill;
2. *Principle of Reinforcement:* Since long the value of reinforcement in the learning process has been acknowledged. It involves teacher encouraging pupils' responses, using verbal praise, accepting their responses or non-verbal ones like a smile. In microteaching lessons, reinforcement encouragement is given

to the student teacher from time to time for his better performance with feedback, as well as he attains satisfaction and his performance is improved. Reinforcement and feedback stimulate him for better learning and better teaching;

3. *Principle of Experimentation*: Microteaching was born in an experiment. Experiment consists of objective observation of action performed under controlled conditions. Therefore, controlled conditions are necessary in microteaching. The student teacher and supervisor conduct experiment on teaching skill under controlled conditions. Variables such as time, content, students, and teaching techniques may be manipulated or controlled. Since the very beginning, microteaching has been used as a means of research. Those aspects of microteaching that render it valuable as a training also valuable as research tools;

4. *Principle of Evaluation*: A proper evaluation of student teachers' work may become an effective motivation for better learning and better teaching. The supervisor evaluates each micro-lesson. In microteaching, self evaluation is also allowed. With the help of video-tape recorder the student teacher may evaluate his own performance. Improvement can be made on the basis of self-evaluation;

5. *Principle of Precise Supervision*: The supervision accompanying microteaching is highly specific and precise. The supervisor pays full attention to one point at a time. Both the supervisor and the student teacher are clear about the aim of micro-lesson ahead of time. The supervisor possesses an 'observation schedule' which he fills in while supervising. He can also make an assessment on a rating scale as rating is a method in which the expression or opinion concerning a particular trait is systematised;

6. *Principle of Continuity*: Microteaching requires continuity. The teacher learns and re-learns the skill of teaching in continuum until he masters it.

Microteaching and Teaching Skills

Teaching is a set of interrelated activities a teacher performs in classroom with a view of facilitating learning in students. Teaching activities can be analysed in terms of teacher behaviour. Teacher behaviour may be considered as a set of activities of the teacher which are observable. The various set of activities of behaviours included in teaching are introducing, explaining, demonstrating, questioning, maintaining classroom discipline, illustrating, encouraging students to answer questions, posing problems for students to solve, etc., which may be described as teaching skills. So, the teaching skills are those interrelated activities of teaching which aim at bringing about desired changes in pupils. This concept of teaching skills has emerged with the advent of microteaching. Therefore, it is widely recognised that the major contribution of microteaching to the present-day teacher education programmes, is the teaching skills.

The following definitions are very much useful to know the significance of teaching skills. Teaching skill is an activity of teaching behaviour of a teacher, used to teach effectively and successfully.

Gage (1968) defines teaching skills as "Technical skills are specific instructional techniques and procedures that a teacher may use in the classroom. They represent an analysis of teaching process in relatively discrete components that can be used in different combination in continuous flow of teacher's performance."

To Merrill (1971), "Teaching skills are instructional interaction skills which the teacher exhibits as a display device."

The Asian Institute of Teacher Educators (1972) has defined 'teaching skills' as "those specific activities of teaching that are effective in bringing about the desired changes in pupil behaviours".

Komisar (1966) has pointed that "various specific activities included in teaching are introducing, citing, hypothesizing, reporting, conjecturing, confirming, contrasting, explaining, questioning, elaborating, etc., which may be considered as constituent skills of teaching.

Brown (1975) defines teaching skills as "as a set of related teaching acts or behaviours performed with the intention to facilitate pupils learning."

B.K. Passi (1976) has defined teaching skill as "a group of teaching acts of behaviours intended to facilitate pupil's learning directly or indirectly."

According to Joyce and Weil (1978), "Teaching skill is a particular teaching behaviour that contributes to the effectiveness and uniqueness of a teaching model."

In the words of Singh (1979), "Teaching skill is a set of teacher behaviour which is especially effective in bringing about desired changes in pupils."

Joshi (1981) defines teaching skill as "a set of behaviours, the occurrence of desirable behaviours and the avoidance of undesirable behaviours either being positively associated or assumed to be associated with certain instructional objectives or change in pupil".

Jangira (1982) has stated a broad-based definition of teaching skill comprising of three levels, viz., component teaching skill, component teaching behaviour, and atomistic teaching behaviour. Based on these levels, teaching skill is a set of interrelated component teaching behaviour for the realisation of specific instructional objectives.

Menon, et al. (1984) define teaching skill as "a group of behaviours which can be developed through practice and be used in an equally efficient manner in situations other than these utilised for its practice".

McIntyre and White have defined teaching skill as "a set of related teaching behaviours which in specified type of classroom interaction situations tend to facilitate the achievement of specific type of educational objectives".

A systematic review of literature reveals that a large number of teaching skills have been identified by various researchers in India and abroad.

The first attempt made in this regard, at the Stanford University in USA by Allen and Ryans (1969) suggest fourteen teaching skills:

- Set induction
- Stimulus variation
- Lecturing
- Silence and Non-verbal eves
- Reinforcing pupil participation
- Recognising behaviour
- Completing the communication
- Fluency in questioning
- Probing questioning
- Divergent questions
- Higher order questions
- Illustrating and use of examples
- Planned repetition
- Closure

Likewise, Passi and his associates (1976) have identified the following teaching skills:

- Writing Instructional Objectives
- Introducing lesson
- Using Blackboard
- Selecting Content
- Organising Content
- Selecting Audio-visual Aids
- Recognizing Attending Behaviour
- Increasing Pupil Participation
- Silence and Non-verbal Cues
- Fluency in Questioning
- Probing Questions
- Explaining
- Illustrating with Examples

- Reinforcement
- Remedial Measures
- Stimulus Variation
- Giving Assignments
- Evaluation
- Achieving Closure

Jangira and his associates (1979) in their attempt to identify various teaching skills have arrived the following list of twenty skills:

- Using Instructional Objectives
- Using Blackboard
- Introducing Lesson
- Stimulus Variation
- Creating a Set for Introducing Lesson
- Selecting a Lesson
- Prompting Pupil Participation
- Organisation of Content
- Evaluating Pupil Progress
- Pacing the Lesson
- Structuring Questions
- Level of Questions
- Illustrating with Examples
- Classroom Management
- Giving Assignment
- Using Verbal and Non-verbal Cues
- Response Management
- Diagnosing and Providing Remedial Measures
- Explaining
- Achieving Closure

Singh (1979) has identified the following nine teaching skills:

- Stimulus Variation
- Reinforcement
- Reacting
- Quality of Questioning
- Probing Questioning
- Silence and Non-verbal Cues
- Explaining
- Liveliness
- Recognising and Achieving Attending Behaviour

Paintal (1980) has identified the following skills:

- Introducing Lesson
- Lecturing
- Using Blackboard
- Stimulus Variation
- Silence and Non-verbal Cues
- Illustrating with Examples
- Reinforcement
- Using Audio-visual Aids
- Explaining
- Closure

Similarly, Menon and his associates (1983) have provided the following list of teaching skills:

- Skills of Planning and Preparation
- Skills of Presentation of Communication
- Skills of Guidance and Counselling
- Skills to Work in Team
- Leadership Skills

- Organisation Skills
- Skills of Organising Group Interaction
- Problem Solving Skills
- Evaluation Skills.

Joshi and his associates (1985) have identified the following teaching skills:

- Set Induction
- Reinforcement
- Stimulus Variation
- Use of Aids
- Reacting
- Explaining
- Narration
- Illustrating with Examples
- Using Blackboard-I
- Using Blackboard-II
- Questioning (basic)
- Questioning (open/closed)
- Questioning for Feedback
- Probing Questioning
- Closure

The course of study prescribed for B.Ed. students of Dibrugarh University involves 8 teaching skills as follows :

- Writing Instructional Objectives
- Introducing a Lesson
- Blackboard Writing
- Questioning
- Stimulus Variation

- Explaining
- Demonstration
- Achieving Closure

NCERT in its publication Core Teaching Skills (1982), has laid stress on the following teaching skills:

- Writing Instructional Objectives
- Organising the Content
- Creating Set for Introducing the Lesson
- Introducing the Lesson
- Structuring Classroom Questions
- Questions Delivery and Distribution
- Response Management
- Explaining
- Illustrating with Examples
- Using Teaching Aids
- Stimulus Variation
- Pacing of the Lesson
- Promoting Pupil Participation
- Use of Blackboard
- Achieving Closure of the Lesson
- Giving Assignments
- Evaluating the Pupils Progress
- Diagnosing Pupil Learning Difficulties and Taking/Remedial Measures
- Management of the Class

Ram Babu (2007) has identified the following teaching skills:

- Writing Instructional Objectives
- Selection and Preparation of Teaching Aids

- Introducing a Lesson
- Reinforcement
- Demonstration
- Stimulus Variation
- Illustrating with Examples
- Use of Blackboard
- Explaining
- Fluency of Questioning
- Probing Questioning
- Closure
- Use of Teaching Aids
- Mapping
- Listening
- Speaking
- Reading
- Writing
- Line Practice (integration of teaching skills)

J.C. Aggarwal has defined component teaching skills associated with different stages of lessons.

I. *Planning Stage*

Component Teaching Skills

- Selecting the Content
- Organising the Content
- Writing Instructional Objectives
- Selecting Audio-visual Material

II. *Introductory Stage (Set-Induction)*

Component Teaching Skills

- Creating Set for Introducing the Lesson

- Introducing the Lesson

III. Presentation Stage

Component Teaching Skills

(a) Questioning Skill

- Structuring Classroom Questions
- Fluency in Questions
- Different Types of Questions
- Use of Higher Order Questions
- Divergent Questions
- Distribution of Questions
- Response Management

(b) Presentation Skills

- Pacing the Lesson
- Lecturing/Narration
- Explaining
- Demonstrating
- Discussing
- Illustrating with Examples

(c) Aids Using Skills

- Using Aids
- Using Blackboard
- Stimulus Variation
- Silence and Non-verbal Cues
- Reinforcement

(d) Management Skills

- Promoting Pupil Participations
- Recognising Attendance Behaviour
- Managing the Class

IV. Closing Stage

Component Teaching Skills

- Achieving Closure
- Planned Repetitions
- Giving Assignment
- Evaluating the Students' Progress
- Diagnosing Students' Learning Difficulties and Taking Remedial Measures.

L.C. Singh describes some of the skills which may be described with the help of microteaching:

1. ***Stimulus Variation:*** Stimulus variation is related to classroom attention. It is based on the principle that changes in the stimuli in one's perception capture his attention. This skill involves deliberate change of various attention catching behaviours by the teachers in order to keep pupils' attention at high level. Such behaviours include teacher movements, gestures, change in speech patterns, focusing, changing interaction, style, shifting sensor channels, pausing and such others;

2. ***Set Induction:*** There term set means the establishment of cognitive report between pupils and teachers to obtain immediate involvement in the lesson. Teaching experience indicates a direct relationship between the effectiveness in inducting set and effectiveness in the total lesson. If the teacher succeeds in creating a positive set, the likelihood of pupil involvement in lesson is enhanced;

3. ***Closure:*** Closure is complementary to 'set induction'. Its attained major purposes, principles and constructs of a lesson or portion of lesson are judged to have been learnt and the pupils are able to relate new knowledge with the past. It is not only a summary of the portions covered. It brings a cognitive link between past and new knowledge if pupils feel a sense of achievement. If the planned lesson is not completed, the teacher may use closure by drawing attention to the major points accomplished unto that point;

4. *Teacher's Silence and Non-verbal Cues:* Teacher's silence and non-verbal cues is a powerful tool in the classroom. During silence, deliberately introduced by the teacher, he uses some non-verbal cues like gestures, body movements, etc., in order to encourage pupil participation;

5. *Reinforcing Pupil Participation:* Reinforcing desired pupil behaviour through the use of positive reinforcing behaviours is an integral part of learning process. This skill requires the teacher to encourage pupils' responses or any desirable behaviour by using verbal statements like "good", "continue", etc., or non-verbal cues like a smile, nodding the hand, etc.;

6. *Fluency in Questioning:* Fluency is a skill in asking questions. It means the use of as many questions as possible in a given period of time. However, no question is found to be relevant unless it is followed by effective student responses. The purpose behind this skill is to increase the number of meaningful questions asked by the teacher in a given period of time keeping in view its effectiveness;

7. *Probing Questions:* This skill requires that the teacher asks questions that requires pupils to go beyond superficial 'first answer' questions. This may be done in five ways: (i) asking the pupil for more information and/or more meaning; (ii) requiring the pupil to rationally justify his response; (iii) refocussing the pupil's or class's attention on a related issue; (iv) prompting the pupil or giving him hints; (v) redirecting the question to other pupils;

8. *Recognising and Attending Behaviour:* Teachers may be trained to become more sensitive to the class-room behaviour of pupils. Through visual cues, a successful teacher quickly notes indication of interest or boredom, comprehension or bewilderment. Facial expression, directions of eyes, the tilt of head, and boldly posture, etc., offer common recurrent cues which make it possible for the skilled teacher to evaluate his classroom performance according to the pupils' reactions. Now, he may change his 'pace' of the very activity, introduce new instructional strategies as necessary, and improve the quality of his teaching;

9. ***Illustration and Use of Examples:*** For good, sound and clear teaching, the use of examples is basic. Examples should be given to clarify, verify, or substantiate concepts. Both inductive and deductive types of examples may be used by teacher effectively. This effective use of examples included: (i) starting with simple example and progressing to more complex ones; (ii) starting with examples relevant to student's experiences and knowledge; (iii) relating the examples to the principles or ideas being taught; (iv) checking to see if the objectives of the lesson have been achieved by asking students to give examples which illustrate the main point;
10. ***Explaining:*** An explanation in a classroom is a set of inter-related statements made by the teacher related to a phenomenon, an idea, etc., in order to bring about or increase understanding in the pupils about it. To become an effective explainer in the class room the teacher should practice more and more of desirable behaviours such as using explaining links, using beginning and concluding statements and testing pupils understanding behaviours like making irrelevant statements, lacking in continuity, using inappropriate vocabulary, lacking fluency, and using vague words and phrases;
11. ***Increasing Pupil Participation:*** Increasing pupil participation involves integration of four components, viz., creating set, questioning, encouraging pupil participation and pausing in such a way that pupil participation is maximised. Pupil participation involves pupils' verbal response and initiation. The first three components of the skill involve both verbal and non-verbal behaviours.
12. ***Using Blackboard:*** Blackboards are used for the: (i) Writing legibly on the blackboard using distinctly different letters which are large enough to be read by all pupils and with adequate space in between them; (ii) Keeping the blackboard neat which can be achieved by retaining only the relevant matter under focus and by ensuring that there is no over-writing; and (iii) Appropriateness of written work on the blackboard. This means brevity, simplicity, and continuity in the points being

present, underlining the important facts with coloured chalks, developing the necessary and proportionate diagrams along with the lesson, etc.;

13. ***Writing Instructional Objectives:*** Writing instructional objectives is viewed as writing objectives in such a way that they may be: (i) well stated ; (ii)adequate with respect to learning outcomes; (iii) relevant to the content; and (iv) adequate with respect content outline;

14. *Class Management:* This skill involves teaching consisting of a number of functions or activities that teacher performs as an integral part of the teaching job, i.e., creating conditions within the classroom group as well as in the classroom environment which enables students to behave in socially approved ways, and makes learning interesting, calling and appealing;

15. *Using Audio-visual Aids:* Learning is made more meaningful, interesting and effective by audio-visual aids. They attract and hold attention of pupils. They help to combat the tendency of being absent minded. They provide proper motivation, add variety and break the monotony of ordinary instruction. They help in forming the right type of mental images. They stimulate critical thinking and increase the power of receptivity. Audio visual aids are most effective when they aim at supplementing class teaching. While selecting the instructional materials, the teacher must consider the knowledge of the pupils, the subject matter to be taught, the situation in which they are presented, the time at hand, and the ability to handle and use aids;

16. *Giving Assignment:* An assignment is a task or piece of work given by a teacher to an individual student or to a class. It is always a part of the daily lesson plan of the teacher. Properly understood, skillfully planned, intelligently assigned and sympathetically checked assignments are indispensable and invaluable. Teacher's skill of giving assignment consists in motivating the pupils in order to awaken interest, defining the objectivities in clear and simple terms, setting proper time limits, and supervising the given assignment;

17. ***Pacing the Lesson:*** The skill of pacing of a lesson means the variation in the speed of teaching. It should depend commonly upon the amount of difficulty experienced by the pupils in mastering the lesson. Several problems in teaching may be easily solved if adequate attention is paid by the teacher to allocate the time needed to every lesson. The teacher should keep in mind the following points: While packing the lesson; the time at hand; the syllabus to be covered; the level of mental ability of pupils, and the objectives of the lesson to be taught. He can know the pace of the lesson by recognising the attending and non-attending behaviour of the pupils. On the basis of this, the pacing can be increased or decreased.

18. ***Use of Higher Order Questions:*** Higher order questions are questions which cannot be answered either from memory or simple sensory description. Such questions call for finding rule or principle rather than defining one. The basic critical requirement for a good classroom question is that it prompts the student to use ideas rather than just remembering them. Although, some teachers intuitively ask questions of high quality, but too many over-emphasise those that require only the simplest cognitive activity on the part of students. Procedures have been designed to sensitise novice teachers to the effects of questioning on their students and provide practice in forming and using higher order questions;

19. ***Divergent Questions:*** A divergent question is that which involves higher order thinking, the answer to which are not predictable and more than one in number. It requires the respondent to organise elements into new patterns, predict hypotheses or to infer from situations. Such questions provoke pupils to higher order thinking in the classroom so that from a long-term view they may develop higher order skills such as those involved in problem solving;

20. ***Lecturing:*** The skill is training in some of the successful techniques of lecturing based upon a communication model. It includes delivery techniques, use of audio-visual materials, set induction, pacing, closure, redundancy and repetition, and other skills related to lecturing;

21. *Planned Repetition:* The purpose of planned repetition is to clarify and reinforce the ideas, key words, principles and concepts in a lecture or discussion. The use of this skill is a powerful technique in focussing and highlighting important points, and describing them from different point of view. Improper use of planned repetition may cause confusion and poor learning among the students. On the other hand, its proper use may direct their attention to points which the teachers wish to emphasise;

22. *Completeness of Communication:* Although the importance and need for complete communication is blatant, it is not often the guiding principle in actual communication. The focus of this skill is sensitivity training on the importance and the difficulty of being understood. Classroom games had been devised which dramatically demonstrate to teachers that what they consider to be clear instructions are often not clear at all to students. Sensitivity training in the skill of communicating with others will create teachers who are more responsive to possible miscommunication.

Modern Categories of Basic Skills in Teaching

The following broad categories of basic skills in teaching have been given by Modern Experts:

1. *Planning Skills:* This includes skill of writing instructional objectives;
2. *Motivation Skills:* These skills include encouraging pupils, set induction and establishing rapport;
3. *Presentation Skills:* These skills include introducing a lesson, explaining the lesson, giving examples, lecturing, drilling, using blackboard and other aids;
4. *Questioning Skills:* These include fluency in asking questions and probing questions;
5. *Skill of Small Group Instruction:* This class of skill includes programming or individualising instruction, guiding and counselling;

6. ***Developing Pupils' Thinking:*** Developing pupils' thinking includes developing thinking, reasoning, problem solving, creativity and self-direction;
7. ***Evaluation Skills:*** These skills include skills of assessment, diagnosing of difficulties and providing remedial measures;
8. ***Managerial Skills:*** These skills include skill of class-management and maintaining discipline.

Role of Supervisor in Microteaching

R.N. Sharma says that microteaching supervisor is essentially a teacher. His role is to increase and refine performance of the skills that serve as the objectives. The responsibilities of the supervisor in microteaching are mentioned hereunder:

1. *Developing Ability to Perform a Skill:* The supervisor should help the trainee develop ability to perform a skill. The supervisor discharges the following functions in this role: (i) The supervisor helps the trainee in discrimination of the skill and reinforces his performance of it; (ii) The supervisor tries to understand the behaviours that constitute the skill and to become sensitive to that signal when the skill should be performed; (iii)The supervisor reinforces his behaviour where the trainee performs the skill or begins to approximate the performance of it;
2. *Making understanding the Application of Skill:* The supervisor could help the trainee to understand as to where the skill should be applied. Having a repertory of reinforcement skills does not ensure good classroom application. Good performance depends on when and where the skills are used. The supervisor, therefore, must help the trainee in making professional decisions;
3. *Working with Trainees:* Each supervisor is assigned between 6 to 10 teacher trainees at the start of the session in microteaching and he works with this group;
4. *Visiting Schools*: The supervisor visits his trainees in the school and prepares a special schedule of microteaching lessons in the practicing schools. This requires special arrangements. The

period allowed is only between five to ten minutes. The pupils discuss with the supervisor after the lesson;

5. *Supervising the Lesson*: The supervisor supervises the lesson. He notes the improvements which are to be made by the pupil-teacher in the presentation of the lesson;

6. *Evaluating the Lesson:* The supervisor evaluates the lesson and gives feedback.

J.C. Aggarwal states that "a supervisor plays a leading role in microteaching. He assists student teachers in relating component skills of teaching both to theory underlying the skills and to practical classroom situations. The supervisor has to provide continuous consultation so that he can help the student teacher transfer the skill learnt in microteaching setting to the actual classroom. First of all, he gives demonstration of a particular skill and thereafter, he prepares a special schedule of microteaching lessons in the practicing schools. He supervises the lesson and discusses with the student teacher in a group of other student teachers. He completes the evaluation schedule and gives the feedback. The supervisor is expected to work hard to be a model for the student teachers."

Evaluation Instruments

The teaching skills developed through microteaching lessons should be evaluated by the peers or supervisors. The rating scheduled is used as criterion measure. Stanford Teacher Competence Appraisal Guide (STCAG) is the most popular evaluation instrument for assessing the effectiveness of microteaching.

Allen and Ryan (1969) have given the following evaluation sheet for assessing the skill of reinforcement. This consists of four dimensions of the reinforcement skill:

1. *Rewarding Correct Response:* The correct responses of the students could be praised or rewarded by saying 'fine', 'good', 'excellent', etc.;

2. *Using Non-verbal Cues:* To encourage students, the teacher should use non-verbal eves such as smile, etc.;

3. *Giving Credit:* The teacher should give credit to students answering a question partly correct;

4. *Referring to Positive Aspects:* The teacher should refer to positive aspects of student's previous responses.

The observer records these four dimensions in terms of frequency that the teacher has used the category number of times. The categories are assessed on scales ranging from three to seven points. The STCAG consists of a number of scales rating the broad aspects of a teacher's performance.

Aids and Apparatus in Microteaching

The following aids and apparatus are used in microteaching:

1. *Observations Schedule (Check List)*: The observation schedule may be used in the form of checklist or questionnaire. It should include all items to be observed;
2. *Cassette Tape Recorder:* A cassette tape-recorder may be used for recording the entire conversation in the classroom. It can be used for appraising one's own self or by supervisor;
3. *Video Tape Recorder*: Use of video tape recorder has both the advantages of sight and sound;
4. *Closed Circuit Television:* The entire classroom programmes can be seen in another room and shown to other group through closed circuit television while it is taking place. Thus all the staff members and teachers can see the lesson without disturbing the class with the help of closed circuit television;
5. *Movie Film*: The entire programme can be recorded with the help of a movie film which can be seen again and again;
6. *One-way Screen*: One way screen may be used for some purposes;
7. *Two Monitors*: Two monitors should be available for assistance.

Advantages of Microteaching

Microteaching is distinguished by the following advantages as explained by R.N. Sharma:

1. *Modification of teacher behaviour*: Microteaching is an effective device for the modification of teacher behaviour;

2. *Knowledge of teaching skills:* By the use of microteaching the knowledge and practice of teaching skills can be given;
3. *Developing teaching skills*: Microteaching experiences develop the specific teaching skills such as reinforcement skill, explaining skill, skill of using black board, skill of using audio-visual aids, skill of class management, etc.;
4. *Developing teaching efficiency:* Microteaching is found useful for developing teaching efficiency in pre-service and in-service teacher education programmes;
5. *Improving teaching practice*: This technique is a training device for improving teaching practice and prepare better and effective teachers;
6. *Individual training:* By microteaching the training of teacher becomes individualised. Each trainee makes progress in developing teaching skills at his rate depending on his ability;
7. *Regulating teaching practice*: The technique permits increased control and regulates teaching practice;
8. *Real teaching*: Microteaching is real teaching. It may be one either in real class room condition or simulated conditions;
9. *Reducing complexities*: Microteaching reduces the complexities of normal classroom teaching by scaled down teaching, class-size, scope of content, and time;
10. *Focus on teaching:* Microteaching focuses attention on teaching behaviour to modify and improve in the desired directions;
11. *Analysing one's own teaching performance:* This technique is an economical device and the use of video-tape enables the trainee to analyse his own teaching performance;
12. *Continuous reinforcement*: In microteaching, the mechanism of feedback devices can be combined with other device such as simulated social skill training and interaction analysis device which provide continuous reinforcement to the trainee's performance;
13. *Research tool*: In the end, microteaching is a useful research tool which may be used by the teacher candidates to study teaching even during their training;

J.C. Aggarwal states the following advantages:

1. Microteaching is real teaching;
2. Microteaching lessens the complexities of normal class room teaching;
3. Microteaching focuses on training for the accomplishment of specific tasks;
4. Microteaching allows for the increased control of practice;
5. Microteaching greatly expands the normal knowledge of results of feedback dimension in teaching;

A. Ram Babu (2007) states the advantages of microteaching as:

1. Microteaching is training for real teaching;
2. It paves way for macro-lesson;
3. It is an increased control of practice;
4. Feedback is immediately given;
5. Specific skills can be developed by microteaching;
6. Teaching under simulation conditions is also possible;
7. This technique is more useful for the training of one or more skills;
8. It simplifies the study of interaction between the teacher and the pupils;
9. It develops integration of theory and practice;
10. It helps in the research work related to classroom teaching;
11. It provides for self-evaluation through the tape recorder and videotape;

Usha Rao proposes the advantages of microteaching as:

1. There comes a major awareness to pupil teachers with regard to professional training;
2. There is more scope for practice in teaching skills according to the student's potential;

3. It develops confidence by having the practice of skills in microteaching under simulated conditions;
4. It creates more general teaching competence among the pupil teachers;
5. It allows for different strategies for supervisory feedback;
6. It helps to identify categories in which additional research is needed;
7. It helps in improving the methods of criticising student's performance;
8. It determines the length of training time required to master certain skills;
9. It helps in improving the ways of analysing pupil-learning;
10. It focuses attention on teacher behaviour;
11. It offers opportunity to practice a real lesson without the complexities of a normal classroom;
12. It offers several sources of immediate feedback;
13. One skill is learn at a time;
14. It equips the beginner with an array of teaching skills before he/she faces the real classroom situation;
15. Evaluation procedure of a micro-lesson is more precise, objective and acceptable;
16. Major steps of a micro-lesson are towards individualizing the training of teachers;
17. It helps in the development of self-confidence;
18. It helps in getting acquainted with classroom manners to a certain extent;
19. It helps the trainees to develop the skill of blackboard writing;
20. It is helpful in improving his/her own teaching;
21. It introduces precise technical terms useful to the teacher for discussion at the professional level;
22. It makes trainees familiar with various teaching styles, e.g. blackboard writing, use of aids, asking questions etc.;

K.L. Kumar suggests the following advantages of microteaching:

1. It is more manageable than classroom teaching. This is because the number of persons involved is only 5-10 and the duration of teaching is 5-10 minutes only;
2. It permits concentration on some specific skill(s) to be demonstrated. All observable, demonstrable and quantifiable skills are within the scope of microteaching;
3. It operates in a healthy environment where only the fellow teachers and colleagues are present;
4. It enables a student teacher to view and hear his/her own performance and thus enable him/her to make self criticism;
5. It permits senor teachers to assist the younger teachers to identify their strengths and weaknesses in a practical manner and hence set guidelines for improvement;
6. Second and subsequent cycles of microteaching result in further critical analysis and improvement in teaching skills;

N. Ananthakrishan explains the following advantages of microteaching:

1. It focuses on sharpening and developing specific teaching skills and eliminating errors;
2. It enables understanding of behaviours important in classroom teaching;
3. It increases the confidence of the learner teacher;
4. It is a vehicle of continuous training applicable at all stages not only to teachers at the beginning of their career but also for more senior teachers;
5. It enables projection of model instructional skills;
6. It provides expert supervision and constructive feedback and above all if provides for repeated practice without adverse consequences to the teacher or his students.

Limitations of Microteaching

In spite of the above advantages, microteaching suffers from the following limitations, as per R.N. Sharma.

1. *Costly*: An effective microteaching system requires tape-recorder, video-tape recorders and / or closed circuit television. Therefore, it is costly for Indian schools;
2. *Narrow scope*: Microteaching provides opportunities for developing only a few skills (say 20 to 25). However, in reality, the teaching requires more than these skills;
3. *Disturbs existing time-table*: Microteaching disturbs the existing time table of practicing schools by calling small group of students for a few minutes (say five or ten);
4. *Presentation in parts*: A very small content is presented. This in five or ten minutes separates or breaks the lesson;
5. *Difficulty in actual practice*: Microteaching is difficult in actual practice in a class of 5 to 10 pupils. The pupil teacher may not get any difficulty. He may gain a lot of confidence. But in a class of fifty or more, he may fail to teach;

J.C. Aggarwal states the following limitations of microteaching:

1. For successful implementation, microteaching requires competent and suitably trained teacher-educators;
2. Microteaching tends to reduce the creativity of teachers;
3. Microteaching can be carried on successfully in a controlled environment only;
4. Microteaching is very time consuming;
5. The application of microteaching to new teaching practices is limited;
6. Microteaching alone may not be adequate. It needs to be supplemented and integrated with other teaching techniques;

A. Ram Babu (2007) found the following limitations of microteaching:

1. Microteaching does not take into consideration the overall environment of teaching;

2. It is a skill-oriented technique instead of being content-oriented;
3. It has limited scope for developing skills;
4. It does not provide broad-based behaviours in terms of skills;
5. In training colleges, microteaching lab is very expensive;
6. It requires video recorder, tape recorder and other devices for making the micro-lesson very effective. It becomes difficult for training colleges to make such arrangements;
7. Experts in microteaching are generally scare;
8. It needs sufficient time to impart the teaching skills among all the student teachers;
9. It is alone not enough to attain perfection in teaching. It will be effective if supported with interaction analysis and simulated teaching method.

According to Usha Rao the limitations of microteaching are:

1. *Administrative difficulty:* No school will readily allow to have only 5 to 10 pupils from each class for practicing a micro-lesson;
2. Lack of material resources and trained supervisors;
3. Cannot be a substitute for real classroom lesson;
4. Sufficient literature on microteaching is not yet available;
5. Microteaching under simulated conditions does not affect the development of general teaching competence;
6. Teaching cannot be broken down into sub-components as they lose meaning in isolation and teaching is not a combination of these isolated bits;
7. Teaching task is not to produce skills as an end in themselves but as a means to an end;
8. Teaching is not just a summation of teaching skills;
9. By itself, microteaching is not a substitute for any other teaching method, but it is just a supplement to other methods.

K.L. Kumar states the following limitations of microteaching:

1. It is only a simulated technique with less number of persons over a short period of time. The classroom performance of the same teacher could be much worse (sometimes better!) since there are larger number of students over a longer span of time;
2. It is expensive to procure and to maintain video recording equipment just for microteaching;
3. It is usually limited to lecturing; extension to laboratory teaching, tutorials, cybernetics, etc., need to be explored;
4. It is conducted under controlled environment where different audio-visual resources, etc, are provided. Real-life situations are quite different;
5. Microteaching technique applies only to observable, demonstratable and quantifiable skills. It does not apply to other skills such as decision-making, preparation of audio-visual resources, maintaining student records, etc.;

N. Ananthakrishan criticises the microteaching in following way:

Lack of adequate and in-depth awareness of the purpose of microteaching has led to criticisms that microteaching produces homogenised standard roots with set smiles and procedures. It is said to be a form of play acting in unnatural surroundings and it is feared that the acquired skill may not be internalised.

However, these criticisms lack substance. A lot depends on the motivation of the teacher to improve himself and the ability of the observer to give a good feedback. Repeated experiments abroad have shown that, over a period, of time microteaching produces remarkable improvement in teaching skills.

Improvement of Microteaching

The following programme highlights the strategies to improve teaching through microteaching:

Health professionals acknowledge that their education does not prepare them for teaching. However, society's increasingly high expectations on health professionals demand that they be taught and trained effectively;

Health professionals who want to improve their teaching competency can take up microteaching at the National Teacher Training Centre for the Health Professions (NTTCHP) at the University of the Philippines. The following is the description of the experience of 3 batches of students with regard to how the course affected their delivery skills;

This is an action research programme that documented how the teaching competency of students improved after experiencing microteaching. Study samples included classes in the first semester of 2005-2006 (Batch 1=9), the second semester of 2002-2003 (Batch 2 = 11) and the second semester of 2000-2001 (Batch 3=12). Written and oral (anecdotal) reports and evaluations of students' performance were used. All data were originally collected as part of the course requirements but were later collated as part of the course requirements and reviewed for the Third Asia-Pacific Medical Education conference. All the data were analysed qualitatively for patterns, trends and descriptions;

Microteaching refers to a "scaled-down teaching encounter designed to develop new skills and refine old ones". It involves a simulated teaching session where students practice teach in laboratory that involve a faculty supervisor, the demonstrating teacher, peers, a video supervisor, video recorder and player and a television monitor.

This is consistent with the teach-reteach cycle described by Trott. It consists of: (1) the briefing phase; (2) the preparation phase; (3) the teaching stage; (4) the review by the class and supervisor; and (5) either preparation for the next session or a reteach of the same skill.

The gains in microteaching depend on how the teacher demonstrators reflect and improve on their skills after formal evaluation and personal introspection.

Results and Discussion

In the degree programme of the Master in Health Professions Education, offered by the NTTCHP, HP 241: practicum or microteaching is a compulsory, 2-unit laboratory course of 4 hours per week for 16 weeks.

The 3 batches of 32 students included in the study were faculty members, whose teaching experience ranged from 1 semester to 25 years. By profession, 56 per cent of the students were physicians, 25 per cent were dentists, 12.5 per cent were physical therapists, while nurses and radiological technologists made up 3.12 per cent each.

Briefing Stage

Initially, each class underwent an orientation and desensitisation stage. These involved exercises in overcoming their fear of standing in front of camera, encouraging them to depend on and build each other's confidence and developing themselves as a functional learning group.

Preparation Stage

The students formulated their own instructional designs and the teaching-learning scenarios they would present in class using an identified basic skill which they would demonstrate. The delivery skills that were identified include:

1. arousing and sustaining motivation;
2. explaining clearly;
3. questioning effectively; and
4. managing difficult students.

The class constructed an evaluation instrument that listed competency in each skill according to the minimum pass level and the relevant principles in teaching and learning.

Teach/Reteach Stage

At this stage, the students delivered their lessons in a scaled down teaching session which took between 5 and 25 minutes.

The first teaching sessions were the most stressful to students because of the fear of criticism. They felt that having their classmates as their simulated students was superficial to the setting as these students would later assume the role of peer reviewers.

Of the 32 students in this study, 2 demonstrated motivational skills only once. They did not have to reteach again and proceeded to the next skill. On the other hand, all had 2 demonstration sessions to explain, question, facilitate, and establish closure. Those who underwent the second session markedly improved their presentations. None of the students demonstrated the same skill thrice.

Viewing and Analysis of Sessions

Viewing and evaluation began with self-appraisal on the good and bad points observed, improvements to be made, and whether the presentation met the minimum standard. The other students and faculty supervisors then offered their own observations.

The classes appreciated the value of scaled-down teaching encounters. They analysed the physical, psychological, and emotional aspects of the teaching act.

For motivation, students considered the use of interesting and innovative cases, problems or pictures, maintaining a warm and challenging environment, dressing up for the part and variation in gestures.

All classes recognised the fact that explaining was basic to teaching. Presentations were critiqued based on organisation and discussion of concepts, citation of appropriate examples and the ability to ask questions. The use of signposts, foci and links were monitored to establish integration.

The students also improved their explanation techniques by transferring difficult topics into learnable units, 2. using advanced organisers, 3. integrating the lecture with applications on topics that span the cognitive and psychomotor learning domains, and 4. using of questions and pauses. Voice modulation, enthusiasm, use of modern instructional media and maintenance of rapport were considered during the review. Students appreciated how they changed their behaviour on and off the camera.

Debriefing Stage

This final stage in the teach-reteach cycle took place after each student completed a skill. The students summarised the skills completed. The final debriefing session was almost always held on the last day of class on the 16th week and a final commendation was made of each student. A comment made by one of the earlier students was often quoted in this debriefing session. Microteaching made them better teachers because the experience afforded them time to look at themselves in a non-threatening setting.

Conclusion

Microteaching, a laborious and intensive practice teaching experience at the NTTCHP improved the teaching competence of the course participants.

Guidelines for Preparation for a Good Microteaching

A micro-teach is an 8-10 minute lesson in which you will put into practice the elements of effective teaching. At registration you will be assigned to a small group of eight to ten other teacher associates (TAs). You will work with this group during portions of the orientation and will do your microteaching with them. Each group will be led by a faculty member or experienced TA.

You will present your lesson with your group members serving as students. The presentations will be videotaped. You will view them and critique your own videotape using the principles learned in the orientation. Your private replay and self-analysis will be followed by a one-on-one conference with your group leader. The conference will help you identify strength in your presentation and provide suggestions for the areas you would like to improve.

Microteaching provides you with an opportunity to 'get your feet wet' in teaching before you go into your first class session, laboratory, tutorial, or other interaction with students. Every year new TAs tell that the micro-teach was the most valuable part of the orientation.

Teaching Fellows Talk About Microteaching

Marc Scheff, Junior in Computer Science

Marc was a first-time undergraduate Teaching Assistant (TA) for CS 51 in the spring of 1998. Because he missed the two TA meetings held by the course during intercession, and every TA was required to receive some form of teacher training, he decided to sign up for microteaching "so I wouldn't jump into section fully unprepared," he says, "Let's say I had some crazy problem with teaching—I'd rather know before I get into the first section." Because there was no course-wide microteaching scheduled, Marc signed up for a microteaching session with the help of the DEAS student coordinator.

One of the advantages of microteaching, Marc feels, is that "you get some hands on - experience—you actually do what your job is." Because the two other TAs involved in the microteaching session and the consultant, John Girash, were not in Computer Science, he says, "It was interesting to try to explain some ideas that I find pretty simple to somebody who didn't have much of a concept of what I was talking about." Marc felt comfortable receiving feedback from his peers and thought their comments were fair. "People are all in the same boat," he explains, "so they are willing to give you fair and accurate criticism because they want the same." As a first-time teacher, Marc also found John's comments especially helpful. "Not only his comments to me," he says, "but his comments to other people — I watched and I said, 'Oh, that's something I've got to watch out for,' or 'Oh, that's interesting to look for.'"

A week after the microteaching session Marc watched his teaching segment on tape with John. He was not surprised by anything on the tape, he says, "Because I feel like when you know you're under a scrutinising, critical eye you are critical of yourself during the process. You're also over-criticising yourself because you don't want to give other people the chance to — you'd rather catch it yourself." Still, he did notice some things that he felt he did well and some he thought he could do better.

Though Marc feels he did not learn anything earth-shattering in the microteaching session, he found the comments very helpful. "Even if it was a little comment," he says, "'This was good because you did this,' or even 'This wasn't so bad but you could do this better,' that's really helpful." Marc also thinks that it might be useful for people to see themselves teaching on tape more than once, "Because," he says, "they might just hold their breath and see it once and deal with it." As someone in a singing group who watches each concert on videotape afterwards, he explains, "It's useful to see yourself on a regular basis." Marc recommends microteaching to all TAs and TFs, adding, "I feel like even some of the more experienced

Teaching Fellows (TFs) would benefit occasionally from something like this, though they may not admit it."

Adam Fagen, G-5 in Biology, Society and Education, an Ad Hoc programme

All the TFs for the course Adam taught—BS 1—were required to participate in a microteaching session, even if they had teaching experience, as was the case with Adam, who had taught twice before but had received no formal training. Adam liked the fact that the head TF made a point of mentioning at the start of the microteaching session that it was designed to help rather than to "police" TFs. He feels that this point should be emphasised by those leading the sessions to make TFs more comfortable with the process.

Adam prepared two topics from the list the TFs were given and decided to do the more hands-on of the two in the session because it was something he hadn't done before. Although he can't remember saying anything positive about his own teaching at the session, the other TFs had only positive comments for him. He explains, "We always think 'Oh, I'm just not doing well' when you're up there teaching and it's nice to hear people say, 'No, No. I thought that was actually good.'" The main comment people had about his teaching, Adam remembers, is that he seemed very accessible and that students would feel comfortable asking him questions without feeling stupid.

The most useful aspect of microteaching for Adam was the chance to see himself teaching. He feels that seeing oneself in the role of teacher is an important step. "When I was teaching the first time," he says, "it took me a few weeks just to realise 'Okay, I'm up here, I don't know why, but I am and that's all there is to it." While microteaching may have helped him realise this role sooner the first time he taught, he feels that it helped him on a different level at this point in his teaching career. He was able to concentrate less on subject material and more on how it comes across to his students. He adds, "For me it was just useful to see that I'm actually doing better than I might have expected."

Because of his low expectations, Adam was pleasantly surprised when he watched himself teaching on videotape. "I was a lot more effusive and energetic and dynamic than I feel myself being," he says. So the experience turned out to be a validation of what he was already doing, but also a reminder to do certain things he feels he doesn't do enough. Adam also found watching the tape with a consultant very useful. He says, "Having somebody sitting there who's seen a lot more of these techniques and things, you can say, 'Did that make sense?' or 'Do you know a better way I could do that?'". There were also specific things that the consultant suggested Adam focus on and see how they went during the semester.

Another benefit of microteaching for Adam was having a chance to talk about teaching with his colleagues. Because he feels that there is not enough attention paid to teaching, especially in the sciences, Adam says, "It was encouraging and useful to start the dialogue about different techniques that you can use." This dialogue continued throughout the semester. Having a microteaching session at the outset, Adam says, "makes for a very collegial atmosphere; we try to help each other out and provide suggestions when they're useful."

Olivia Johnson, Center for Astrophysics

Olivia, a recent graduate of Vassar working at the Center for Astrophysics, had never taught before receiving a Teaching Assistantship for Science A-35. She and her fellow TAs and TFs, even those who had done microteaching before, were required by the course head to participate in a microteaching session. Participants were told to prepare seven minutes of a class they would teach during the first week. "I remembered a problem I had learned my freshman year in astronomy class," Olivia says, "about comparing the stars in the sky with the number of grains of sand on the beach and it's a nice concise problem, so I chose it."

Olivia was very nervous about teaching, especially because she was not a graduate student and had never taught. But the experience of standing up and teaching at the microteaching session actually eased her nervousness and served as a reminder, she says, "that I do know what I'm doing and that I know the subject." Olivia was thankful that she had the chance to practice teaching before going into a real classroom. "I used an overhead projector, which I'd always done in undergraduate consortiums," she explains, "and it was a dismal failure for trying to teach a problem, so probably within the first half-minute I knew that was not the way I was actually going to teach a class." Even so, she felt that she had done better than she'd expected, which boosted her confidence. Watching herself teach on videotape served as a further confidence-builder. She hadn't really believed the consultant when he had told her she did not look nervous teaching, but when she saw the tape for herself she had to agree with him.

Olivia found the comments on the other TFs teaching extremely helpful. "There were lots of things," she says, "as a first-time teacher that I'd never thought about. I learned a lot about using blackboards and I also learned a number of ways of getting students more involved that I wouldn't have thought about." She also thought it interesting to hear different ideas about teaching methods. She says, "I guess there's a main philosophy here which is 'get your students involved,' but the ways in which different people had planned to do it — it was interesting to hear the variation."

As with Adam's course, the dialogue among TFs initiated at the microteaching session continued throughout the semester. "I think it probably helped in getting us to know each other," Olivia says, "and also to let each of us see the level of our surroundings. As someone who isn't a graduate student and hasn't had any sort of introduction to teaching, it was reassuring to see that everyone else there was doing the same caliber stuff I was, and I think that probably helped me to talk more in TF meetings, knowing these people weren't going to say, 'You fool!"

Sam Dyson, Center for Astrophysics

Sam, who did his undergraduate work in physics at Yale, was a TA for the same course as Olivia, and so was also required to participate in the microteaching session. Sam had spent the year after his college graduation teaching high school in South Africa, and then had taught several sessions for an introductory physics course at Yale.

Though Sam had teaching experience, he had never had any formal teacher training. He says, "One of the things I really liked about microteaching is that it got us ready for the semester of TA-ing by really dealing with the methods of teaching and the session we had was very real. And it was very good to have the feedback of other people who will be in the same position, who were able to put themselves in the place of students — it really made you think about how your approach would be received by students." Sam also liked the fact that everyone, including the teacher, had to say something positive first. He says, "You don't often think about what you did well and what you enjoyed and I'm sure that it assured a lot of people before the first section."

Sam felt the feedback he received was extremely helpful. He was glad to hear that people enjoyed his fun, easy-going style which developed during his year of teaching high school students. But through one of the consultant's comments he realised that his self-deprecating manner might sometimes go too far. When he introduced himself to the "students" he said, 'I'm an astrophysicist, but, you know, that term is a bit lofty for me, I'm not all that.'" He realised that making jokes at himself for comic relief might make his students doubt him.

Sam watched himself on tape with the consultant immediately after the session. In addition to confirming the comments above, the tape made Sam aware of his tendency to rush through a lesson because, he says, "I believed that the whole thing is summed up and made valuable by the final sentence or conclusion and not by the method along the way." Something he saw that he felt good was that he asked the "students" their names. "Because of that," he says, "I spent a lot of time at the first section and the next one with the students thinking about their names, really trying to remember who they were."

Sam feels that microteaching is a good way for teachers to prepare themselves for their first day of sessions. As teaching high school served as an ice-breaker for him, Sam says, "I think in the same way microteaching really just relaxes people and if they come away with no other constructive criticism or positive feedback, at least they have their nerves slightly more under control and that is a really good thing." He adds, "I think good things come from it. It gives an air that what we are doing is important. It conveys the sense that teaching is not something you do because you know the material, that that doesn't qualify you to be a teacher. And I look forward, if I'm ever TA-ing again, to doing it again".

Elizabeth Ross, G-2 in fine Arts

Liz calls herself "the great experiment" in her department because she is the only graduate student — in student memory — to teach as a G-2 and while still taking courses. The course she was teaching - Landmarks in World Architecture — did not organise a microteaching session because, Liz says, all the other TFs had taught before. It was only after Mary-Ann had suggested microteaching to Liz that she found out that she was actually required to do some kind of training as a first-time teacher. Mary-Ann organised a microteaching session for Liz and one other TF teaching an introductory Fine Arts course (Silvia Foschi). Because there were only two TFs involved, Mary-Ann recruited two undergraduates to act as students during the teaching segments and to offer feedback.

The microteaching session took place the day before Liz's first section, "So that was very good," Liz says, "because Mary-Ann got me in there very fast and I managed to do it before I actually had to go in front of a real-live audience." However, she adds that if it had not been a positive experience, it would have been a bad idea to have it the day before her first session.

Liz was nervous about teaching because she is not much older than the students and architecture is not her field, so much of what she was teaching was also new to her. Though she felt comfortable with the lesson plan for the first session because it was "tried and true," having been used for years in another architecture course, Liz was worried that the students would realise that she was teaching from a script. Therefore, in the microteaching session, she says, "It was very positive to have undergraduates say, 'We liked the way this worked pedagogically,'" and she was pleased when they were surprised to learn that she was following a script. Because the undergraduates responded well to the lesson, Liz says, "I didn't have that fear that I was going to walk into the section and have people be quiet."

Liz felt that the microteaching session was not enough to completely assuage all her fears because she had only taught the beginning of one lesson and the sessions would inevitably become more complicated. Furthermore she wondered whether the positive comments had more to do with the script than with her teaching.

Therefore, a few weeks later she had Mary-Ann follow up on the microteaching with a visit to her section. While she thinks of microteaching as a positive experience which gave her confidence to go in and teach her first session, she says, "I remember when Mary-Ann came to the section as being a more constructive and critical exercise, so the two went in tandem."

When asked whether she would recommend microteaching to other TFs, Liz says, "Yes, for first time TFs it gives confidence and then to follow through with having someone sit in on your section is good." She also thinks microteaching could benefit TFs who have already taught, because they might fall into patterns and stop evaluating themselves. She adds, "Anything that keeps you thinking about your session as opposed to just doing them each week—not just 'what am I going to do in there for an hour?' but 'How am I going to do it' — is a good thing."

Silvia Foschi, Visiting Scholar at the Graduate School of Design

Silvia, a visiting scholar from Italy teaching LA B-39 (Michelangelo), participated in the same microteaching session as Liz. Though she had taught many times during her doctoral programme in Italy, Silvia had never taught in America; therefore, she was required to go through some kind of training. She participated in the Bok Center's Teaching in English Programme, which, she says "was absolutely useful to me because I couldn't understand the American system — we don't have sections in Italy and we don't have that kind of close relationship with students — not at all." When Mary-Ann suggested Silvia do the microteaching as well, she felt that the more she learned about teaching in the American classroom beforehand, the better.

In Italy, Silvia was accustomed to lecturing her students, of whom, she says, "it is required that they know something about history, art historical language, art, so I start my lecture without thinking that they don't know something because they have to know it — it is absolutely up to them." Therefore, leading a discussion among students with widely differing backgrounds was something completely new to her. She found it very useful to get feedback on her teaching before she went into the real classroom and she didn't feel criticised, she says, "because I realised that it was something that I needed."

Silvia watched herself teaching on tape twice, once during the Teaching in English Programme, and then after the microteaching session. She remembers the first time being struck by how serious she looked while teaching. She felt that she had to change, "because I have to be more friendly with my students," she says, "especially because they are so young and so scared by art." She also realised that she had to open up a dialogue with her students. She explains, "At the beginning I was more focussed on my field, on what I had to say, to teach, and now I think it's more important to let them speak." Though Silvia did not comment on this herself, Mary-Ann recalls Silvia's surprise at seeing herself using more body-language to explain things in English than she does in Italian. Mary-Ann adds, "This was really effective when she was trying to explain the difference between high relief and low relief sculpture — the students responded to that very positively."

Like Liz, Silvia felt that just as helpful as the microteaching session were the follow-up meetings with Mary-Ann during the semester. She says, "I worked with her in order to prepare every section — she helped me all the time." Not only did they talk about each section beforehand, they also discussed how it went afterwards.

Though Silvia feels that as a foreign TF it was "absolutely useful" for her to receive teacher training in order to learn a new system, in general, she says, "I don't think that you can learn to teach. It's something that you have inside yourself — maybe I'm very Italian in this. You can improve, but not learn." And she explains, "The best way to improve yourself is experience." However, Silvia does say that she will take some of the things she learned about teaching at Harvard back to Italy with her, adding, "I want a more direct relationship with my students — absolutely."

RESEARCH STUDIES

Following are the research findings related to microteaching.

Microteaching and Feedback

Shah (1970) reported that the listening to the tape-recorder lessons helped the teachers in correcting the mistakes.

Acheson (1964) noticed that video feedback as against no feedback produced significant differences for teacher monologue, but there were no significant differences between any of the supervisory variables.

Tuckman and Oliver (1968) reported that: (i) The pupil feedback did produce a significantly greater change in teacher behaviours than supervisory feedback; and (ii) Supervisory feedback alone also produced changes in teacher behaviour.

Department of Education, Excter (1971) found that: (i) Interaction analysis feedback reduced the amount of straight lecturing as does television, where as no feedback tended to increase it; and (ii) After interaction analysis feedback, there was increase in the children participation.

Wragg (1971) reported that the combination of video playback and interaction analysis could be a powerful means both for influencing behaviour and for increasing competence in the teaching act.

Young (1970) noticed that students working in teams performed a significantly greater number of specific teaching behaviours in orienting student to the learning task.

Young, Lee and Rechords (1971) reported that there is no significant difference between the feedback of video and oral groups.

Sharma (1977) found that there is no differential effect of three treatments was discussion, oral and written techniques of feedback upon the attainment of the skill of gestures.

Sharma (1976) reported that audio as well as supervisory feedback was more effective in developing skill of questioning.

Weeks (1973) observed that feedback video tape self-concentration and systematic pupil feedback produced no important difference in the student teacher attitudes.

Department of Education, NCERT (1976-77) reported that there was no significant difference between the scores of groups getting supervisory feedback and peer feedback.

Stronck (1975) claimed that students rated performance poorer than did peers.

Passi (1977) reported that significant difference between the acquisition of general teaching competence by student teachers having the treatment of instructional material and skill based feedback and student teachers of the control group.

Bhagia and Bhouwraskar (1977), Dixit (1977), Prajapati (1977), Rama (1977), Vishesharao (1977) and Pillay (1977) observed that the feedback given by peers and by supervisors had similar effects on development of general teaching competence.

Pangotra (1973) reported that the student teachers who received self directed feedback performed better than those who received feedback from other sources.

Ray (1978) stated that the performance of teachers trained through microteaching for skill acquisition either under supervisory feedback or with supervisory-cum-audio tape feedback was significantly higher the gain scores of general competence than that of the filler group.

Paikaray (1979) reported that there was no significant difference between the means of control group and other two experimental groups which were provided feedback by peer and audiotape.

Passi, et.al. (1980) found that the peers' feedback was significantly more effective than self-feedback through audio tape in the development of general teaching competence among the secondary school level student teachers.

Paikary (1981) reported that there was no significant difference between the means of control group and experimental group that were provided feedback by peer and audiotape.

Singh (1982) stated that the control group and the experimental group, i.e., groups which received feedback given by peers, supervisors, and self-feedback had similar effects on the development of general teaching competence.

Hooda and Syag (1984) reported that the extrovert peer supervisors were superior in their feedback performance to the introvert peer supervisors.

Hao (1990) reported that the students who received the correct feedback had modified their undesirable verbal teaching behaviour more effectively than did students in both the treatment-non-corrective and the control groups.

Purohit, Z.N. (1987) noticed that there was no significant difference in microteaching feedback and interaction analysis feedback in bringing about attitudinal change.

Prabhuna, P. P., Marathe, A.H. and Sohani, C.R. (1989) reported that: (i) The difference between the means of the three groups taking three different treatments of feedback were not found to be statistically significant; and (ii) All the three strategies of providing feedback were equally effective.

Dubey, A.S. (1989) reported that the experimental group significantly developed both feedback receiving and feedback giving competencies.

Microteaching and Self Concept

Dosajh (1975) reported that a trend towards direct relationship between intellectual ability and change in teaching self concept is suspected but has not been established for want of enough data.

George and Anand (1980) stated that there was a significant difference between the pre-test and post-test mean teaching self-concept scores of the control group and experimental group of student teachers.

Yogendra Kumar and Rattanlal (1980) reported that microteaching helped the teacher in self assessment of his capabilities, giving sense of self-acceptance and self-achievement.

Microteaching and Personality

Som (1984) reported that: (i) The secondary teachers were neither extrovert nor introvert and they could be tentatively described as lacking patience but possessing sociability, sobriety, carefulness, temporal thought, introspection, concentration and mental exertion, in terms of extroversion and introversion traits; and (ii) Male teachers were found to be more initiating, expressive, careful, introspective, mentally exertive and concentrated than female teachers.

C.S. Dave, (1987) reported that pupils' liking of their teachers was not effected by variation of treatment of teachers' preparation. Instead of present training treatment given to teachers, some other personality factors might be influencing pupils' liking of their teachers.

Microteaching and Intelligence

Kulshreshtha, S.P. (1982) reported that intelligence did not seem to play any significant role in training trainees in two approaches, i.e., mini-teaching and microteaching.

Thakkar (1985) found that than there was no correlation between intelligence and effect of microteaching skills upon general teaching competence.

Microteaching and Teaching Skills

Chudsama (1971) reported that microteaching helps in the development of questioning skill and increased pupil participation in the lesson.

Marker (1972) reported that microteaching was a better technique than the conventional approach in the development of certain teaching skills, namely, set induction, stimulus variation, questioning and closure.

Joshi (1974), Passi and Shah (1974) noticed that the microteaching was effective in developing the skills of questioning reinforcement, non-verbal cues, and illustration with examples.

Abrahm (1974) reported that the microteaching technique was effective in developing the skills of fluency in questioning and probing questioning.

Joshi (1977), Lalita (1977), and Passi (1977) observed that microteaching was more effective than traditional approach in developing the skills, namely, skill of writing instructional objectives, introducing a lesson, fluency in questioning, probing questioning, explaining, illustrating with examples, stimulus variation, silence.

Sharma (1976) reported that microteaching in developing the skill of questioning in pre-service teachers is a very effective technique.

Perrott (1976) stated that there were a number of clear and stable changes in patterns of questioning behaviour.

Passi (1977) reported that the two experimental groups trained in clusters of skills differed significantly from the group having traditional teacher training.

Ray (1978) reported that: (i) The in-service teachers reacted favourably towards the techniques of skill acquisition; and (ii) The performance of teachers trained through microteaching for skill acquisition under self-analysis through audio tapes was as effective as teachers in the filler group.

Pattanshetti (1985) indicated that microteaching (SIMC) was found effective in improving the orientation skill, the skill of explaining, stimulus variation, and achieving closure of college teachers.

Kalyanpurkar (1986) reported that microteaching treatment held a positive and significant effect on the development of skills, viz., probing questioning, reinforcement, explaining with examples and stimulus variation.

Schur (1991) reported that microteaching is an effective means of providing instructors with new teaching skills and techniques.

Pratap, D. (1982) found that the student teachers of the microteaching groups had a higher level of ability to use the learnt skill in an integrated form in normal classroom settings than the control group had.

Purohit, Z.N. (1981) stated that microteaching helped in the development of various instructional skills.

Sharma, A.K. (1986) noticed that exercise with reinforcement of probing questioning skill behaviour was conductive to growth of a teaching skill.

Arockian, A.S. (1990) reported that teachers improved their questioning skills and the self-learning package was found to be effective.

Chathley, Y.P. (1984) observed that there was a significant improvement in the general teaching competence of trainees as a result of training in microteaching skills.

Yogendra Kumar and Rattan Lal (1980) reported that there was improvement in teaching skills of probing questions, reinforcement, stimulus variation, illustrating with examples, illustrating with aids, increasing pupils' participation after undergoing training through microteaching.

Verma, Bhagwan Swaroop (1988) found that the experimental group showed better competencies in skills like skill of reinforcement, skill of probing questioning, skill of stimulus variation, skill of illustration with examples and skill of explaining.

Pandian, C.C. (1987) observed that science teachers (include mathematic teachers) differed from art and language teachers in their use of stimulus variation, explanation and questioning skill.

Pandya, M.J. (1991) reported tat the student teachers receiving microteaching lessons were significantly better than others taught through traditional techniques on four teaching skills, viz., set-induction, questioning, explaining and blackboard summary.

Microteaching and Locality

Verma, Bhagwanswaroop (1988) reported that the teaching competence of urban student teachers was found to be better than that of their counterpart from rural areas.

Bishnu Charan Das and Bsanta Gogoi (1998) found that there was no significant difference between rural and urban student teachers with respect to their attitude towards microteaching.

Microteaching and Qualifications

Bishnu Charan Das and Basanta Gogoi (1998) reported that there is no significant difference between graduate and postgraduate student teachers with respect to their attitude towards microteaching.

Microteaching and Gender

Som (1984) noticed that female teachers tended to be higher than male teachers in their attitude towards teaching.

Verma, Bhagwan Swaroop (1988) reported that the teaching competency of the female student teachers of the science group was better in comparison to the male student teachers of science group using microteaching approach.

Chathley, Y.P. (1984) reported that: (i) The male trainees having physical sciences gained quantitatively more than their female counterparts. The female trainees in languages gained significantly better than the male ones; and (ii) For the hexaclosted strategy of integration the sex had no impact on the integration of skills.

Bishnu Charan Das and Basanta Gogoi, (1998) noticed that there was no significant difference between male and female student teachers with respect to their attitude towards microteaching.

Microteaching and Teaching Methodology

Jangira, Matto and Sing (1980) reported that the group of 19 in-service social studies teachers included in the study showed significant gains in the mean scores on the competence to use the five teaching skills, namely, reinforcement, probing, stimulus variation, illustrating with examples and increasing pupils' participation after their training using microteaching.

Jangira, Singh and Matto (1981) found that microteaching technique brought about significant improvement in teaching skill competence and general teaching competence of science teachers.

Ashija (1982) reported that microteaching had an advantage over conventional teaching practice in developing skills specific to teaching modern mathematics.

Naik (1984) stated that the experimental group scored significantly higher than the control group when tested for gain in application of objectives in physics and physics and chemistry together.

Khan (1985) reported that student teachers treated with the technique of skill based microteaching were found to be more effective in general teaching competence than those trained in traditional method of teaching English.

Oak (1985) concluded that: (i) While training the science and mathematics student teachers, activities such as teacher talk, questioning, blackboard work, and demonstration should be taken into account in preferential order; and (ii) Mathematics teachers needed training in order of priority in activities such as explaining, questioning and blackboard work.

Chatley, Y.P. (1984) reported that: (i) The trainees in physical science gained more in overall general teaching competence than their counterparts in social sciences and languages; and (ii) All the 12 skills under study, the trainees in physical science gained significantly more than the trainees in social sciences and languages.

Pratap, D. (1982) observed that microteaching had an advantage over conventional student teaching for development of skills specific to teaching modern mathematics.

Verma, Bhagwan Swaroop (1988) reported that there was an effect of training through microteaching approach on the teaching competence of urban student teachers of the science group.

Pandiane, Chandur C. (1987) noticed that: (i) The differences among skills related to mathematics, physics, chemistry and biology teachers differed from history; and (ii) Mathematics and science teachers differed from teachers of history and of Tamil and English in the use of the skill of experience.

Bishnu Charan Das and Basanta Gogoi (1998) reported that there is no significant difference between arts and science student teachers with respect to their attitude towards microteaching.

Microteaching and Block Teaching Practice

Kallenbach (1969) stated that microteaching is a more efficient technique than the block practice training procedures.

Microteaching and Effectiveness of Microteaching

Stanford University (1963) reported that: (i) The microteaching group performed at higher level of teacher competence than the traditionally prepared group; (ii) Trainees acceptance of the value of microteaching was high; and (iii) Significant changes were produced in the performance of trainees of the experimental group.

Stanford University (1966) noticed that the pupil ratings were more reliable than supervisor ratings.

Kallenbach and Gall (1969) reported that microteaching was more efficient than conventional method in that required one fifth of the time and created fewer administrative problems.

Kallenback (1969)observed that experimental group trained through microteaching achieved the same level of proficiency in one fifth of the time taken by the control group.

Bell (1968) reported that, in Home Economics, the microteaching group showed significant gains in teaching performance from initial lesson to final lesson.

Borg (1969) found that significant changes in the behaviour of teachers.

Good Kind (1968) reported that: (i) Greater awareness of specific teaching habits and mannerism; and (ii) Greater awareness of the problem of structuring and pacing in their teaching; and (iii) Greater awareness and use of specific teaching acts and techniques.

Bringham Young University (1966) reported that observing a training teacher's performance globally is much less valuable than observing and helping him to observe one or two specific distrainable actions within the teaching act.

Bloom (1969) reported that: (i) The supervisors who observed the interns were more critical in identifying strengths as well as weaknesses in interns teaching performances possibly because of microteaching clinic; and (ii) The supervisor could see them to be confident while teaching.

McColm and La Dve (1970) found that the student teachers reacted more positively and enthusiastically to their microteaching method courses.

Tiwari (1961) reported that microteaching could be used as a training technique in developing insight in the student teacher and thus making them better teachers.

Khan (1985) noticed that microteaching technique had proved itself to be a more effective teacher training technique than the traditional method when subjected to factorial analysis of variance.

Prabhune, P.P., Marathe, A.H. and Sohani, C.R. (1984) reported that practice of microteaching skill was effective in the improvement of student teacher's performance with respect to teaching.

Pandya M.J. (1991) found that microteaching approach was more effective than the traditional teaching approach.

Gandhi, K.V. (1992) reported that the three variables direct and indirect influence, teacher talk and pupil talk, and microteaching were found to be superior to the traditional approach.

Gor, K.V. (1992) observed that microteaching was a very effective technique.

Das, R.C., et al. (1988) reported that additive intervention proved to be more effective.

Kulshreshta, S.P. and Goswami, S.K. (1982) found that no significant difference between the gain scores on microteaching and mini-teaching approach.

Microteaching and Anxiety

Treese (1972) reported that microteaching was effective in reducing anxiety in female pre-service and secondary school teachers.

Diehlx (1970) stated that teacher comment alone, video tape-record without comment and playback and video-tape record with playback but no comment, resulted insignificantly fewer dissfluences (ow, ah,um, stutter at) than no video-tape.

Hughes (1970) reported that no difference was found on anxiety scores of the two groups of microteaching with lecture method and traditional method.

Sharma (1977) observed that microteaching did help in lowering the state of anxiety level of the student teachers significantly.

Passi, et.al. (1980) reported that the level of anxiety of the secondary student teachers were not affected by specific variations in the different components of microteaching, namely, the feedback, modelling condition.

Microteaching and Achievement

Naik, V.V. (1984) reported that: (i) The C.S. results were not significantly different for gain in the achievement in chemistry, and physics and chemistry together; and (ii) Gain in general teaching competence significantly correlated with gain in achievement in physics as well as chemistry.

Thakkar, R. (1985) noticed no correlation between general achievement and effect of microteaching skills upon general teaching competence.

Khan, A.H. (1985) reported that the analysis of data demonstrated significantly higher effectiveness of microteaching technique in the academic achievement of students in real classroom settings.

Dave (1987) concluded that there was a significant effect of treatment of mini-teaching model of integration in comparison with summative model of integration and traditional model of integration treatments and achievement of pupils.

Purohit, Z.N. (1987) reported that microteaching feedback and interaction analysis feedback produced highly significant gains in the pupil achievement gains in case of interaction analysis.

Microteaching and Teaching Competence

Department of Teacher Education, NCERT (1975) found that trainees trained through microteaching technique acquired high general teaching competence as compared to the trainees trained under the traditional teacher training programme.

Sharma, et.al.(1977) reported that microteaching significantly increased the general teaching competence of teacher trainees.

Jain (1978) stated that the group trained through simulated teaching performs better on general teaching competence than that of trained in real conditions of training.

Joshi (1977) reported that the experimental groups scored higher in the acquisition of general teaching competence than the student teachers exposed to the traditional teaching programme.

GCPI, Allahabad (1977) noticed was no significant difference in the relation of general teaching competence by the two groups, namely, SMT and MMT.

Patel (1978) reported that microteaching treatment in simulated condition was significantly better than the traditional teaching treatment in developing the general teaching competency.

George and Joseph (1978) noticed that the student's reaction to the microteaching approach were positive and favourable.

Kanwal (1979) reported that microteaching helped in developing certain skills in the student teachers thereby increasing general teaching competence.

Passi, et.al (1980) reported that: (i) Microteaching under simulated conditions and under real classroom conditions were equally effective in developing of general teaching competence in the secondary student teachers; and (ii) Development of general teaching competence was not affected adversely when the micro-class size was increased from 9 to 13.

Jangira, Matto and Singh (1980) stated that the teachers showed significant gains in the mean scores on general teaching competence after their training using microteaching.

George and Anand (1980) reported that microteaching proved effective in improving the teaching competence of student teachers.

Bhattacharyjee (1981) found that training for the integration of the four selected skills under the 'summative model' of integration had contributed to the teaching competence of the experimental group significantly in comparison to the control group.

Adeshra (1981) reported that the three groups differed significantly in post-test I in general teaching competence.

Naik (1984) stated that, the experimental group scored significantly higher on general teaching competence than that of control group.

Pattamsetti (1985) reported that a majority of the participant lecturers favoured the SIMC for the improvement of teaching competence.

Kalyan Purkar, S. (1986) found that microteaching treatment had a positive significant effect on the development of general teaching competence.

Dave (1987) reported that the mini teaching model of integration (MMI) was found superior to the summative model of integration (SMI) and traditional model (TMI) of integration in terms of development of general teaching competence in student teachers.

Chathley, Y.P. (1984) noticed that there was a significant improvement in the general teaching competence of trainees as a result of training in micro skills.

Singh, Satyanarayana (1984) reported that the student teachers trained using microteaching under simulated conditions and real classroom conditions acquired better teaching competency than those trained under the traditional training method.

Syag, R.N. (1984) observed that the training approaches of standard microteaching group, traditional student teaching method, and modified microteaching group produced a significant effect on the development of general teaching competence and competencies in specified skills.

Verma, Bhagwan Swaroop (1988) reported that the teaching competency of the student teacher having no experience was better than that of those having experience.

Singh, L.C. (1989) found that the two training strategies were significantly effective in developing general teaching competence.

Singh, H. (1990) reported that meso and microteaching were effective in improving general teaching competence.

Microteaching and Modelling

Bandura, Ross and Ross (1963) found that filmed models are effective as live models.

Orme (1966) reported that: (i) There were differences in effectiveness between symbolic and perceptual modeling; and (ii) Videotape led to significantly greater gains than symbolic modeling.

White (1968) noticed that an audiotape model led to a significant increase in pre-service teachers' use of the indirect behaviour of Flanders's Interaction Analysis Category System.

Claus (1969) reported that modelling accompanied by supervisor's pointing the essential characteristics of the skill proved to be more effective than modelling without any supervisors comments.

Acheson (1974) found that comparisons of pre-and post-training tapes of teaching performance indicated that the variations (i.e., written versus video-tape modelling and audio-tape versus videotape feedback) are equal effectiveness in increasing teacher's use of higher cognitive questions.

Vaze (1975) reported that audio modelling was a better technique when compared to symbolic models for the development of the skills in questioning.

Griffiths (1972) noticed that no significant differences between the group that received perceptual model training and the groups that received supervisor's feedback.

Johnson (1968) reported that different kinds of supervisory behaviours might have differential effects on skill acquisition.

Department of Teacher Education, NCERT (1976-77) found that perceptual and audio-modelling were equally effective in developing skills through microteaching.

Sharma (1977) reported that there is no significant difference between the gain scores of pre and post tests of the experimental and control groups.

Thakkar (1985) found no significant difference between the achievement of the two groups due to two different modes of teaching, viz., the symbolic model and audio-model.

Orme (1966) reported that no significant differences were found between the group that received perceptual model training and the groups that received supervisor's feedback.

Claus (1969) stated that modelling in general was more effective than feedback procedures.

Kantilal Visanji (1992) reported that the symbolic modelling approach and perceptual modelling approach were significantly more effective than traditional approach in developing the teaching competency of primary teacher-trainees.

Microteaching and Attitude

Das, et.al (1977) and Passi (1977) found that microteaching was helpful in changing attitude of student teachers towards teaching.

Ward (1970) noticed positive attitudes towards microteaching.

Perrot and Duthie (1970) stated that the students responded very positively to microteaching and perceived the technique as helpful.

Sharma (1977) found that the attitude of trainees towards microteaching was favourable.

Bhattacharya (1974) reported that the attitude of teacher trainees towards microteaching was highly favourable.

Passi and Shah (1974) observed that the microteaching technique to be feasible and student teachers had developed favourable attitude towards teaching.

Paintal (1980) observed that the six groups had shown a more favourable attitude towards microteaching than Perrott's group of in-service teachers.

Sharma (1986) noticed that pupils' talk response was influenced positively by microteaching treatment.

McCollum and La Dve (1970) stated that the student teachers reacted more positively and enthusiastically to their microteaching method course.

Bell (1970) reported that there was a possibility of a relationship between positive interaction of the group members participating in microteaching and positive attitude towards microteaching.

Singh, Satyanarayana (1984) reported that the microteaching technique mode significant impact in developing a positive attitude in the student teachers towards microteaching.

Pattanshetti, M.M. (1985) reported that the participant lecturers had a favourable attitude towards self-instructional microteaching course materials.

Wadhwa, B.S. (1988) found that microteaching is a functional powerful and valuable instrument useful for teachers.

Verma, Bhagwan Swaroop (1988) reported that the experimental group indicated favourable attitude towards microteaching approach.

Singh, L.C. and Joshi, A.N. (1990) noticed that the experiments conducted in stimulated and real conditions displayed a favourable attitude in the student teachers towards microteaching.

Dutta, Ram (1990) reported that microteaching technique had a positive effect in developing attitude towards microteaching.

Gor, K.V. (1992) reported that microteaching strategies produce significant effect on attitude towards teaching profession.

Department of Teacher Education, NCERT (1966-67) found that results of the studies of 21 institutions showed no change in the teacher attitude towards teaching.

Turney (1970) reported that the trainees' reaction to microteaching was positive and also found that the trainees valued the participation of their peers in the critique sessions.

Joshi (1977) reported that the experimental group did not differ significantly from the control group in its attitude towards microteaching.

Passi, et.al. (1980) reported that attitude towards teaching of the secondary student teachers were not affected by specific variations in the different components of microteaching, namely, feedback and modelling condition.

Ashija (1982) observed that neither microteaching nor conventional practice teaching had any impact on the attitude of student teachers towards teaching.

Wilson (1988) found no significant effects on the attitude measure.

Trent-Wilson (1991) reported that no statistical significance was found in favour of the microteaching programme.

Pratap, D. (1982) found that neither microteaching nor conventional student teaching has any impact on the attitude of student teachers towards teaching.

Asija, Ranveer, Pratap (1990) found that neither microteaching nor the conventional training had any effect on the attitude of prospective secondary school teachers towards teaching.

GCPI, Allahabad (1977) found that the attitude of SMT and MMT groups did not differ significantly from each other.

Passi (1977) reported that all the three groups did not differ significantly among each other in their attitude towards teaching.

Ray (1978) stated that the teachers trained for the acquisition of teaching skills through microteaching under varying sources of feedback did not differ significantly on the gain scores of attitudes from that of the filler group.

Paikaray (1979) reported that there was a significant difference between the attitude scores obtained before and after the experiment of all the groups except for control and audio-tape feedback groups.

Microteaching and Direct or Indirect Behaviour

Bhattacharya (1974) reported that: (i) The audio-recording and microteaching technique would develop successful indirectness among the trainees; and (ii) Microteaching was more effective than conventional technique in the development of indirect teacher behaviour.

Chudasama (1971) found that microteaching was more effective than traditional technique in the development of direct teacher behaviour.

Sharma (1986) reported that incidence of lecturing, the only one among the three direct behaviours decreased consequence of the application of microteaching treatment.

Microteaching and Verbal Behaviour

Singh (1973) reported that student teachers trained through the microteaching technique and through Flanders's Interaction Analysis changed their verbal teaching behaviour more significantly than the student teachers trained through the traditional method.

Sharma (1977) found that microteaching was effective in increasing the use of indirect verbal behaviour of pre-service science teachers.

Rezba (1971) reported that microteaching caused a significant increase in the use of indirect verbal behaviour and significant decrease in the use of lecture.

Singh (1982) reported that the traditional training given to the pupil teachers for control group had no effect on the attitude towards teaching of pupil teachers.

Joshi and Kumar (1983) found that there were no significant gains in attitude towards teaching in both the groups of I and II due to the treatments given.

Dave, (1987) reported that: (i) The teachers belonging to the mini-teaching model of integration group did not attain a significantly favourable attitude towards teaching in comparison to those belonging to the summative model of integration group and traditional model of integration group at occasion II (Post-test-I); and (ii) The teachers belonging to the mini-teaching model of integration group produced significantly favourable attitude towards teaching in comparison to the summative model of integration group and traditional model of integration group at occasion III (Post-test-II).

Syag, R.N. (1984) observed that all the three training approaches SMT, MMT and TST did not produce a significant effect upon the development of the attitude of student teachers towards training.

Microteaching and Classroom Behaviour

Kanwal (1979) reported that the feedback was an important source of variance which modified classroom behaviour, and increased the teaching efficiency of the student teachers.

Kallenbach and Gall (1969) stated that microteaching was not found to be superior to the conventional training methods in its effect of teacher's classroom performance.

Gandhi, K.A. (1992) reported that as compared to the student teachers trained through the microteaching approach, the student teacher through the traditional approach were more direct in their classroom verbal behaviour and showed a narrower percentage of student talk in their classroom behaviour.

Microteaching and Teacher Behaviour

Dosajh (1974) reported that the teacher improved his teaching in all areas through microteaching.

Berliner (1969), Young and Young (1969), Kallern Back (1967), Goodkind (1967), and Wrogg (1971) found that microteaching is effective in changing teacher behaviour in the classroom.

Borg, et.al. (1970) found that decreasing the amount of teacher talk in the classroom discussions, increasing the number of times the teacher uses prompting, and increasing the percentage of total questions that call for higher order pupil cognitive responses influenced the teacher behaviour.

Singh (1974) reported that microteaching was more effective technique as compared to interaction analysis and conventional approaches regarding modifications of teacher behaviour.

Joshi (1984) noticed that the 'Interlinked Microteaching Approach' and the Standard Microteaching' do not differ significantly in their efficiency in changing the teaching behaviour of student teachers.

It is to be concluded, after the study of theoretical perspectives of microteaching and the review of research studies related to microteaching, that a study is required to find out the attitude of prospective teachers towards microteaching.

3

Research Methodology

Research is a systematic enquiry seeking facts through objective and verifiable methods in order to discover the relationship among them and to deduce from them the broad principles or laws. Therefore, the very success of a research work depends upon collecting the necessary information. Several methods of collecting information are developed to assist the research. Every survey expert has his own ideas of selecting the best method of collecting information. But, it can not be uniform to all. Selection of the method depends on the type of information to be gathered and the source of information to be consulted. For the present study, normative survey method is chosen.

Survey means viewing and interpreting things rigorously and comprehensively. Now-a-days, survey method is a popular way of collecting data and analysing the results statistically and systematically. This method is suitable to this study as this one is a status study.

OPERATIONAL DEFINITIONS OF KEY TERMS

The operational definitions of the important key terms used in the present study on " A Study of Attitude of Prospective Teachers towards Microteaching" are discussed and defined herewith:

Study

Study refers to a systematic investigation which is objective and research oriented.

Prospective Teachers

Study teachers studying in colleges of education.

Microteaching

Microteaching is a training technique which requires student teachers to teach a single concept using a specified teaching skill to a small number of pupils in a short duration of time.

Gender

Gender refers to male and female prospective teachers.

Locality

Locality refers to rural and urban prospective teachers.

Attitude

An attitude is an enduring system of positive or negative evaluations, emotional feelings, and action tendencies with reference to a social object or subject.

Methodology

Methodology refers to the method of study under which the student has been admitted into the course. For the present study, arts and science teaching methodologies were considered:

- *Arts methodology*: Where in the student studies Methods of Teaching Social Studies as elective subject;
- *Science methodology*: Where in the student studies methods of Teaching Biological Sciences or Physical Sciences as elective subject.

Educational Qualification

Educational qualification refers to whether the student is a graduate or a postgraduate. For the present study, arts graduates and postgraduates and science graduates and postgraduates were considered:

- *Graduates*: Those who have completed their three year degree course of study in arts or science or commerce as a specialized subject.

- *Postgraduates*: Those who have completed their two year postgraduate course of study in arts or science or commerce as a specialized subject.

VARIABLES OF THE STUDY

Variables are the conditions or characteristics that the experimenter manipulates, controls or observes. There are mainly three types of variables, namely, independent, dependent and intervening. The independent variables are those variables which do not change on manipulation by the experimenter. The dependent variables are those variables which change on manipulation done by the experimenter. The intervening variables are those variables which are dependant both on dependant variables and independent variables.

For the present study, the following independent variables are chosen:

Gender

Male and Female Prospective Teachers;

Locality

Rural and Urban Prospective Teachers;

Methodology

Arts and Science Prospective Teachers;

Educational Qualification

Graduate and Postgraduate Prospective Teachers;

Medium of Instruction

Telugu Medium and English Medium Prospective Teachers.

As the previous studies were contradictory and the selected variables have their key role to play in the formation of attitude towards microteaching, the above mentioned five variables have been chosen for the present study to identify the level and difference of attitude of prospective teachers towards microteaching.

HYPOTHESES OF THE STUDY

Hypotheses are the most important aspects in a research process. It is a tentative supposition or provisional guess which seems to explain the situation under observation. The following hypotheses are formulated based on the variables and objectives of the study. These were stated in "Null hypothesis" form. The null hypothesis states that there is no significant relationship between two or more parameters. It concerns to a judgment at whether apparent differences or relationships are true or whether they merely result from sampling error.

Keeping the objectives in view, the following null hypotheses are formulated:

1. There is no high attitude of prospective teachers towards microteaching;
2. There is no significant difference between the attitude male and female prospective teachers towards microteaching;
3. There is no significant difference between the attitude of rural and urban prospective teachers towards microteaching;
4. There is no significant difference between the attitude of graduate and postgraduate prospective teachers towards microteaching;
5. There is no significant difference between the attitude of arts and science prospective teachers towards microteaching;
6. There is no significant difference between the attitude of Telugu medium and English medium prospective teachers towards microteaching.

SAMPLE OF THE STUDY

A sample is a smaller representation of the larger whole. A sample contains primarily sampling units and a slice of the population representing the universe. A sample must possess the following essential characteristics to provide accurate results. They are representativeness, adequacy, homogeneity, lack of bias smallness in size, accuracy and completeness.

As a sample is a slice of the population, the population for the study refers to all the prospective teachers who undergo one year study during their B.Ed. course in the Colleges of Education.

Sampling is the easiest method of investigation. The purpose of sampling is to draw inferences concerning the universe. According to Cornell, "Sampling is the process by which a relatively small number of individuals are selected or analysed in order to find out something about the entire population or the universe from which it is selected". In any research, various methods are utilised for selection of samples. After a detailed study of all the methods, the stratified random sampling method was selected for the present study.

Stratified random sampling is applied as this method of selection assures each individual element in the universe as equal chance of being chosen. This is suitable for the present study as the universe considered for the study is homogeneous.

In order to reduce the sampling error the sample size of 200 was chosen. In this study, the strata divided are represented in the following table:

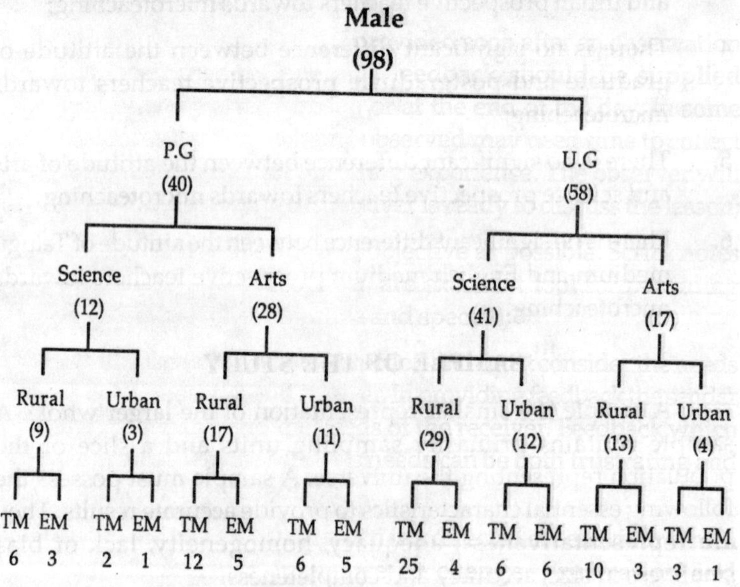

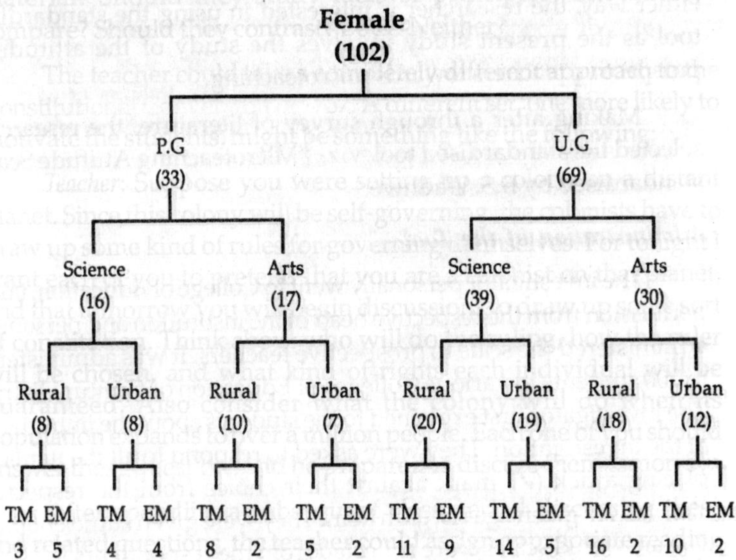

TOOL OF THE STUDY

Research tools are the sole factors in determining the sound data and in drawing accurate conclusion about the problem on hand. The conclusions ultimately help in providing suitable remedial measures to the problem concerned.

The selection and use of tools can be done in two ways. The first one is to construct a tool independently by the researcher for his own study. The second way of selection and use of tool is right selection of tools from already standardised ones available in the field of study. Here also it involves a tedious job in locating the tools and identifying their usefulness to the study on hand. Even then, this technique is very useful when a research work involves a good number of variables and resources are scarce. Some people believe that some of the instruments available don't measure up to their standards. Hence, new ones. In some instances, consideration should be given to the logic of the situation. Lacking the time and financial resources, many researchers can not expect to produce a better instrument. In these cases, the most logical procedure that one can follow is to choose the best instrument available for the purpose.

Considering the flaws and merits of the selection of tools in either way, the researcher is interested in using the standardised tool as the present study involves the study of the attitude of prospective teachers towards microteaching.

Making after a through survey of literature, the researcher selected the standardised tool, viz., "Microteaching Attitude Scale" standardised by B.S. Wadhwe.

Administration of the Tool

The investigator personally went to College of Education, taken permission from the respective head of the institution and personally administered the scale to prospective teachers. It was administered to 200 students in various Colleges of Education of Guntur District. The investigator first explained to the students about the importance of the investigation. They were asked to respond to all the items by placing a tick (✓) mark against their choice from the respective alternatives given against each item. They were given sufficient time. The answered scales were collected from the respondents.

4

Analysis of Data

Analysis of the data is the most skilled task of all stages of research. It depends on the judgment and skill of the researcher. It should be done by the researcher and should not be entrusted to another person. Analysis of data means studying the tabulated material in order to determine inherent facts or meanings. It involves breaking down complex factors into simple ones and putting the parts in new arrangements for the purpose of interpretation.

The first step in the analysis of data is a critical examination of the assembled data. This includes the researcher to think and analyse the data in the next method of analysis, coding. Coding involves assigning symbols to each response, the purpose of which is to translate raw data into symbols. This depends on proper coding of responses. Coding can be done by the respondent or observer or the interviewer. There may be difficulties in coding due to inadequacy of data, inefficiency of the coder and lack of editing or scrutinising of the available data. Editing can be helpful for coding and for improving the quality of data collection.

Tabulation is a means of recording classification in a compact form in such a way so as to facilitate comparisons. Data is arranged in rows and columns to facilitate mathematical and statistical operations. It is of great help in the analysis and interpretation of data, while tabulating the data, the purpose of the study has to be kept in mind.

The method of analysis chosen for a particular study depends upon the nature of objective, hypothesis to be tested, the purpose and use of the study. Statistical methods are mathematical techniques used to facilitate the interpretation of numerical data secured from groups of individual or group of observation or a single individual. A basic knowledge about statistics becomes inevitable for research workers, for systematic analysis and accurate and precise interpretation of data.

For the present study titled "A Study of Attitude of Prospective Teachers Towards Microteaching", several statistical techniques were used to perform the analysis. After collecting the data from two hundred prospective teachers through a standardised tool, the analysis was performed keeping in view the objectives framed, hypotheses formulated, type of data collected, type of tool used, etc. The highest attitude score or the lowest attitude score one can get is 200 or 40 respectively. For this purpose, means, standard deviation, normal probability, critical ratio, etc., were employed.

Hypothesis 1

"There is no high attitude of prospective teachers towards microteaching".

To test the validity of Hypothesis 1, the total scores of the sample were used to calculate the mean and S.D. The results are as follows:

Table 4.1: Level of attitude towards microteaching possessed by the whole sample

Sample	*Sample size*	*Mean*	*Standard Deviation*
Whole	200	152.04	16.64

As per the mean value of the whole sample, the prospective teachers are possessing high attitude towards microteaching.

So, the hypothesis that "There is no high attitude of prospective teachers towards micro teaching" can be rejected.

Hypothesis 2

"There is no significant difference between the attitude of male and female prospective teacher toward microteaching".

The following calculations were made to test the validity of Hypothesis 2. The results are as follows:

Table 4.2: Comparison of attitude towards microteaching between male and female prospective teachers

Variable	*Sample Size*	*Mean*	*S.D.*	*Mean Difference*	*Critical Ratio*
Male	98	148.63	17.08	6.691	2.89*
Female	102	155.32	15.51		

Critical value at 0.05 level is 1.96.

* Significant at 0.05 level.

From the Table 4.2, it is evident that there is a significant difference in the attitude towards microteaching of male and female prospective teachers. Female prospective teachers were having a little bit of high level of attitude towards microteaching than male prospective teachers.

So, the hypothesis that "there is no significant difference between the attitude of male and female prospective teachers towards microteaching" can be rejected.

Hypothesis 3

"There is no significant difference between the attitude of rural and urban prospective teachers towards microteaching".

To test the validity of Hypothesis 3, the following calculations are made:

Table 4.3: Comparison of attitude towards microteaching between rural and urban prospective teachers

Variable	*Sample Size*	*Mean*	*S.D.*	*Mean Difference*	*Critical Ratio*
Rural	124	151.97	15.41	0.13	0.051*
Urban	76	152.11	18.47		

* Not Significant at 0.05 level.

From the Table 4.3, it is evident that both rural and urban prospective teachers were with a high level of attitude towards microteaching without any significant difference between them.

The hypothesis that "there is no significant difference between the attitude of rural and urban prospective teachers towards microteaching" can be accepted.

Hypothesis 4

"There is no significant difference between the attitude of arts and science prospective teachers towards microteaching".

To test the validity of the Hypothesis 4, the following calculations were made:

Table 4.4: Comparison of attitude towards microteaching between arts and science prospective teachers

Variable	*Sample Size*	*Mean*	*S.D.*	*Mean Difference*	*Critical Ratio*
Arts teachers	92	152.67	16.56	1.07	0.45*
Science teachers	108	151.60	16.62		

* Not Significant at 0.05 level.

From the values of Table 4.5, it is clear that arts and science methodology prospective teachers had a high level of attitude towards microteaching without any significant difference between them.

The hypothesis that "there is no significant difference between the attitude of Arts and Science prospective teachers towards microteaching" can be accepted.

Hypothesis 5

"There is no significant difference between the attitude of graduate and postgraduate prospective teachers towards microteaching".

To test the validity of Hypothesis 5, the following calculations were calculated:

Table 4.5: Comparison of attitude towards microteaching between graduate and postgraduate prospective teachers

Variable	*Sample Size*	*Mean*	*S.D.*	*Mean Difference*	*Critical Ratio*
Graduates	127	151.48	16.87	1.31	0.54*
Postgraduates	73	152.79	16.18		

* Not Significant at 0.05 level.

From the values of the Table 4.5, it is evident that graduate and postgraduate prospective teachers were holding high attitude towards microteaching and there is no significant difference between them.

The hypothesis that "there is no significant difference between the attitude of graduate and postgraduate prospective teachers towards microteaching" can be accepted.

Hypothesis 6

"There is no significant difference between the attitude of Telugu medium and English medium prospective teachers towards microteaching".

To test the validity of the Hypothesis 6, the following calculations were made.

Table 4.6: Comparison of attitude towards microteaching between telugu and english medium prospective teachers

Variable	*Sample Size*	*Mean*	*S.D.*	*Mean Difference*	*Critical Ratio*
Telugu Medium	140	151.23	15.28	2.73	0.97*
English Medium	60	153.96	19.31		

* Not Significant at 0.05 level.

From the Table 4.6, it is clear that there is no significant difference in the attitude towards microteaching of Telugu medium and English medium prospective teachers.

So, the hypothesis that "there is no significant difference between the attitude of Telugu medium and English medium prospective teachers towards microteaching" can be accepted.

5

Summary, Conclusions Discussion and Suggestions

Summary

In current practice, however, the student teaching tends to be ineffective. The major defects are inadequate and haphazard supervision, lack of effective models, subjective and global feedback given to student teachers about their teaching performance. In fact, there is no common frame of reference with which supervisors make their observations. They do not have any common model towards which the trainees have to progress during practice teaching. As a result, the trainee remains almost the same in his teaching competence even after the training. In order to meet the challenges and to better teacher education programmes, many innovative practices have been tried out. Microteaching is one of such innovations especially in India (Das, et.al., 1980). It has generated a great deal of enthusiasm in Indian teacher educators and scholars. Microteaching does not involve high cost and is suitable for teacher training programmes. This may be attributed to the fact that:

(i) In microteaching, the teacher education can concentrate on practicing a specific as well as well defined teaching skill and it is easier to practice the skills stated in behavioural terms;

(ii) Microteaching provides for the pinpointed feedback. It is also immediate. Therefore, it is much easier to incorporate than the usual feedback which is delayed and global in nature;

(iii) Microteaching being miniaturised teaching, there is no problem of classroom discipline, so it is a safe practice (Singh, 1979).

(iv) There are less administrative problems in the organisation of microteaching in teacher training institutes because the teaching sessions are arranged with peers. The problems of space and supervisors can also be solved by making skillful arrangement of available facilities (Passi and Shah, 1974).

Further, the findings that teaching through the microteaching is significantly more effective than traditional teaching approach is not only supported by the theories of learning but is also supported by empirical researches.

On the theoretical front, we know that effective learning occurs when active involvement of the learner in the learning process is ensured. In fact, by enabling the student teacher to focus on specific skills, providing immediate feedback from several sources and then allowing him/her to continue practice, microteaching ensures active participation on the part of the student teacher in the learning sessions. Moreover, a student teacher selects his/her own skill of teaching for a micro-lesson and gets oriented with the characteristics of that particular skill. Therefore, by conscious practice of one skill rather than the general practice of teaching, he/she receives a greater chance of practicing and improving upon that skill. This ensures the acquisition of the skill at a time. This practice makes the task much less complex by allowing the student teacher to understand the teaching skill to be learnt and recognise the behaviours that make up the skill.

If microteaching is to be used as an effective technique for teacher training programmes its training strategy should be based on research findings and well tried out practices with available instructional materials developed under Indian conditions. With this idea in mind, it is hoped in this study that its findings would help supplement microteaching to the present day teacher education programmes. Such information could assist policy framers, administrators and teachers to adopt microteaching as an innovative practice in the teacher training programmes for developing teaching efficiency among the student teachers. With these aspects under consideration, the present study is undertaken to study of attitude of prospective teachers towards microteaching.

The objectives of the present study were:

1. To find out the attitude of student teachers towards microteaching;
2. To compare the level of attitude of male and female prospective teachers towards microteaching;
3. To compare the level of attitude of science and arts student teachers towards microteaching;
4. To compare the level of attitude of graduate and postgraduate prospective teachers towards microteaching;
5. To compare the level of attitude of rural and urban prospective teachers towards microteaching;
6. To compare the level of attitude of Telugu medium and English medium prospective teachers towards microteaching;

The normative survey method was used in the present study to investigate the attitude of prospective teachers towards microteaching.

Variables are necessary requisites for any worthwhile research for the purpose of comparison. For the present study, the researcher has considered these variables, viz.:

1. *Location:* Rural and urban prospective teachers;
2. *Teaching methodology:* Science and arts prospective teachers;
3. *Qualification:* Graduate and postgraduate prospective teachers;
4. *Gender:* Male and female prospective teachers; and
5. *Medium of instruction:* Telugu medium and English medium prospective teachers.

Hypotheses are guesses or tentative generalisations which provide basis to the whole study to be tested by facts. For the present study, the hypotheses framed were:

1. There is no high attitude of prospective teachers towards microteaching;
2. There is no significant difference between the attitude of male and female prospective teachers towards microteaching;

3. There is no significant difference between the attitude of rural and urban prospective teachers towards microteaching;
4. There is no significant difference between the attitude of science and arts prospective teachers towards microteaching;
5. There is no significant difference between the attitude of graduate and post-graduates of prospective teachers towards microteaching; and
6. There is no significant difference between the attitude of Telugu medium and English medium prospective teachers towards microteaching.

A sample is a small group which represents all the traits and characteristics of the population. The prospective teachers studying in Colleges of Education of Guntur district were selected as population. The stratified random sampling technique was used in selecting the sample. The sample size was 200 (two hundred) prospective teachers.

A research tool is a tool used for the purpose of data collection. The tool used in the present study was Attitude Towards Microteaching Scale, standardised by B.S. Wadhwa.

For the analysis of data, suitable statistical techniques like mean, standard deviation and critical ratio were used.

CONCLUSIONS AND SUGGESTIONS

The present study has resulted in drawing the following conclusions which may be utilised in improving the attitude towards microteaching of prospective teachers.

The prospective teachers possess a high attitude towards microteaching.

The above result was supported by Ward (1970), Bhattacharya (1974), Parsi and Shah (1974) and Gor, K.V. (1992).

It is a good sign to see a high attitude of prospective teachers towards microteaching. Microteaching is a very important aspect in B.Ed. course which develops the teaching skills individually at mastery level among prospective teachers. Even though there are moderate facilities related to microteaching in Colleges of Education, the prospective teachers possessed high attitude towards microteaching by making the best use of them. Use of proper methods and ability of the teachers in creating real interest among the prospective teachers in learning of microteaching skills develop positive attitude. With this right attitude, if utilised properly, these prospective teachers become good professionals in teaching in future.

The male and female prospective teachers are having a high level of attitude towards microteaching with a significant difference between them.

The above result is supported by Som (1984), and contradicted by Bishun Charan Das and Basanta Gogoi (1998).

The personality, mental as well as physical maturity, surrounding environment, aspirations and aptitudes, etc., might have played their legitimate role in having a significant difference in the level of attitude towards microteaching of male and female prospective teachers.

The teacher educators have to develop an equal and high attitude of prospective teachers towards microteaching.

The rural and urban prospective teachers are possessing high level of attitude towards microteaching without any significant difference between them.

The above result is supported by Bishnu Charan Das, Basanta Gogoi (1998), and contradicted by Verma, Bhagwan Swaroop (1988).

Generally, it is believed that urban prospective teachers due to their exposure to many aspects like infrastructure facilities, congenial teaching-learning atmosphere, good teacher student interaction, easy accessibility to library, etc., can possess high positive attitudes towards microteaching. But, now-a-days, rural prospective teachers were showing themselves equivalent to the urban prospective teachers due to the facilities provided to them like good transportation, trained teachers in colleges, good facilities, proper teaching material, etc. So, there is no significant difference in the attitudes of rural and urban prospective teachers towards microteaching.

This trend should continue so as to how good teachers in our rural and urban schools to prosper perfectively.

The Science and Arts prospective teachers are having a high level of attitude towards microteaching with no significant difference between them.

Though the science and arts students perceive and have a different kind of knowledge of general education and teacher education, both of them have similar level of course work in teacher education. It is really a good sign that the science and arts prospective teachers are having high attitude towards microteaching.

As the microteaching component is common for both arts and science prospective teachers, they should excel in similar in regular schools after their appointment as teachers.

The graduate and postgraduate prospective teachers are possessing high level of attitude towards microteaching without any significant difference between them.

Usually, people feel that there will be much difference between the attitude of postgraduate and graduate prospective teachers towards microteaching as postgraduate prospective teachers may have higher mental development than that of graduate students. Now-a-days, most of the postgraduates are interested to go software side. But, due to parental pressure, many of them came to this profession. Whereas graduates might have interest in this teaching profession. In the present study, both graduate and postgraduate prospective teachers are having high level of attitude towards microteaching without any significant difference between them.

This trend needs to be continued so that the schools get skilled teachers to impart education with ease and effect.

The Telugu medium and English medium prospective teachers are having high level of attitude towards microteaching with no significant difference between them.

It is happy to know that the Telugu medium and English medium prospective teachers have high positive attitude towards microteaching without any significant difference between them. Even though the student strength of Telugu medium prospective teachers are high, but their attitude towards microteaching is at the lower side as compared to that of English medium prospective teachers who are less in number, though not at significant level.

All the teachers should possess all the teaching skills and do well in schools.

SUGGESTIONS FOR FURTHER RESEARCH

The present study on attitude of prospective teachers towards microteaching brings to light a good number of new areas to be studied by the future researchers. The areas and variables which are not covered by this study may be put to test to enlighten the factors associated with the inculcation and development of attitude towards microteaching. So, the researchers may think of the following areas to study in details:

1. There is a need to study the effectiveness of microteaching in relation to other variables like achievement, aptitude, intelligence, thinking pattern, etc.;
2. Investigations can be undertaken to evaluate the conditions for the success of the microteaching in the classroom;
3. Feasibility of the microteaching of the school and college level can also be studied as is followed in advanced countries in training classes;
4. Comprehensive, organised and instructional attempts should be made to identify specific skills required in special settings or for different levels and different subject, while doing so, however, clear distinction should be made between general and specific teaching skills;
5. Attempts should be made to produce self-instructional materials on general teaching skills in different regional languages;
6. Comparative studies with new training techniques or innovations may be continued along with microteaching;
7. Efforts should be made to validate the teaching skills so far identified in terms of pupil achievement.

BIBLIOGRAPHY

ACS Summer Teaching Workshop — What is Microteaching?—Online Document.

Agarwal, J.C. (1999). *Essentials of Educational Technology: Teaching Learning Innovations in Education*. New Delhi: Vikas Publishing House Pvt. Ltd.

Ananthakrishnan, N. (January, 2008). *Microteaching as a Vehicle of Teacher Training: Its Advantages and Disadvantages*. 39(3); 142-143.

Best, John W. and James V. Khan (2005). *Research in Education*, 9th Edition. New Delhi: Prentice-Hall of India Private Limited.

Bishnu Charan Das and Basanta Gogoi (2004). *Micro Teaching*. New Delhi: Kalyani Publishers.

Buch, M.B., Editor (1978-1983). *Third Survey of Research in Education*. Baroda: CASE, M.S. University of Baroda.

Buch, M.B., Editor (1983-1988). *Fourth Survey of Research in Education*. New Delhi: NCERT.

Buch, M.B., Editor (1988-1992). *Fifth Survey of Research in Education*. New Delhi: NCERT.

Derek Bok Center for Teaching and Learning, Harvard University (August 15, 2007), *Microteaching — 'Wikipedia, The Free Encyclopaedia*.

Derek Bok Center for Teaching and Learning, Harvard University. *What is Microteaching*. Online Document.

Derek Bok Center for Teaching and Learning, Harvard University. *Teaching Fellows Talk About Micro Teaching*. Online Document.

Dwinght W. Allen and Weiping Wang (2007). *Education Encyclopaedia: Microteaching*.

Erlyn Aclan Sana. *Improving Teaching Through Micro Teaching*. Manila: University of the Philippines.

Iris, Paintal (1980). *Microteaching — A Hand Book for Teachers*. New Delhi: Oxford University Press.

Jagannath, Mohanty (2004). *Modern Trends in Educational Technology*. Hyderabad: Neelkamal Publications Pvt. Ltd.

Materials for Microteaching – Online Document.

Microteaching. Guidelines for Advanced Preparation – Online Document.

Murthy, S.K. (1984). *Educational Technology*. Ludhiana: Prakash Brothers.

Ram Babu, A. (2007). *Essentials of Microteaching*. Hyderabad: Neelkamal Publications Pvt. Ltd.

Sharma, R.N. (1992). *Principals and Techniques of Eduction*. New Delhi: Surjeet Publications.

Siddhu, Kulbir Singh (1990). *Methodology of Research in Education*. New Delhi: Sterling Publishers Private Limited.

Singh, L.C. (1979). *Microteaching — An Innovation in Teacher Education*. New Delhi: NCERT.

Usha Rao (1997). *Educational Technology*. Mumbai: Himalaya Publishing House.

Additional Reading

Bhaskara Rao, Digumarti (1994). *Scientific Aptitude*. New Delhi: Ashish Publishing House. ISBN 81-7024-658-X.

Bhaskara Rao, Digumarti (1995). *Animal Kingdom*. New Delhi: Discovery Publishing House. ISBN 81-7141-274-2.

Bhaskara Rao, Digumarti (1995). *Batracology*. New Delhi: Discovery Publishing House. ISBN 81-7141-279-3.

Bhaskara Rao, Digumarti (1997). *Scientific Attitude*. New Delhi: Discovery Publishing House. ISBN 81-7141-381-1.

Bhaskara Rao, Digumarti (1996). *Scientific Attitude vis-à-vis Scientific Aptitude*. New Delhi: Discovery Publishing House. ISBN 81-7141-308-0.

Bhaskara Rao, Digumarti (2004). *Scientific Attitude, Scientific Aptitude and Achievement*. New Delhi: Discovery Publishing House. ISBN 81-7141-781-7.

Bhaskara Rao, Digumarti (2004). *Educational Administration*. New Delhi: Discovery Publishing House. ISBN 81-7141-842-2.

Bhaskara Rao, Digumarti (2004). *Issues in School Education*. New Delhi: Discovery Publishing House. ISBN 81-8356-025-3.

Bhaskara Rao, Digumarti, Editor (1996). *Encyclopaedia of Education For All*, 5 Volumes. New Delhi: APH Publishing Corporation. ISBN 81-7024-759-4 (set).

Vol. I *Education For All: The World Conference*. ISBN 81-7024-760-8.

Vol. II *Education For All: The EPA-9 Summit*. ISBN 81-7024-761-6.

Vol. III *Education For All: Quality Education For All*. ISBN 81-7024-762-6.

Vol. IV *Education For All: Planning and Monitoring*. ISBN 81-7024-763-4.

Vol. V: *Education For All: The Indian Scenario*. ISBN 81-7024-764-0.

Bhaskara Rao, Digumarti, Editor (1996). *National Policy on Education*, 2 Volumes. New Delhi: Anmol Publications Pvt. Ltd. ISBN 81-7488-323-1.

Bhaskara Rao, Digumarti, Editor (1996). *Global Perceptions on Peace Education*, 3 Volumes. New Delhi: Discovery Publishing House. ISBN 81-7141-319-6.

Bhaskara Rao, Digumarti, Editor (1997). *Education for the 21st Century*. New Delhi: Discovery Publishing House. ISBN 81-7141-389-7.

Bhaskara Rao, Digumarti, Editor (1997). *Reflections on Scientific Attitude*. New Delhi: Discovery Publishing House. ISBN 81-7141-319-6.

Bhaskara Rao, Digumarti, Editor (1997). *Success Story of a Primary Education Project*. New Delhi: APH Publishing Corporation. ISBN 81-7024-850-7.

Bhaskara Rao, Digumarti, Editor (1997). *World Food Summit*. New Delhi: Discovery Publishing House. ISBN 81-7141-386-2.

Bhaskara Rao, Digumarti, Editor (1997). ***Care the Child***, 2 Volumes. New Delhi: Discovery Publishing House. ISBN 81-7141-394-3.

Bhaskara Rao, Digumarti, Editor (1998). *Earth Summit*, 2 Volumes. New Delhi: Discovery Publishing House. ISBN 81-7141-435-4.

Bhaskara Rao, Digumarti, Editor (1998). *Adolescence Education*. New Delhi: Discovery Publishing House. ISBN 81-7141-432-X.

Bhaskara Rao, Digumarti, Editor (1998). *Community and School Nutrition Education*. New Delhi: Discovery Publishing House. ISBN 81-7141-435-4.

Bhaskara Rao, Digumarti, Editor (1998). *District Primary Education Programme*. New Delhi: Discovery Publishing House. ISBN 81-7141-396-X.

Bhaskara Rao, Digumarti, Editor (1998). *National Policy on Education: Towards an Enlightened and Humane Society*. New Delhi: Discovery Publishing House. ISBN 81-7141-426-5.

Bhaskara Rao, Digumarti, Editor (1998). *Reforming School Education*. New Delhi: Discovery Publishing House. ISBN 81-7141-403-6.

Bhaskara Rao, Digumarti, Editor (1998). *Teacher Education in India*. New Delhi: Discovery Publishing House. ISBN 81-7141-406-0.

Bhaskara Rao, Digumarti, Editor (1998). *World Summit for Social Development*. New Delhi: Discovery Publishing House. ISBN 81-7141-420-6.

Bhaskara Rao, Digumarti, Editor (1999). *International Encyclopaedia of AIDS*, 11 Volumes. New Delhi: Discovery Publishing House. ISBN 81-7141-522-6 (set).

Vol. 1 *Introduction to HIV/AIDS*. ISBN 81-7141-523-7.

Vol. 2 *HIV/AIDS – Issues and Challenges*, 2 Parts. ISBN 81-7141-524-5.

Vol. 3 *HIV/AIDS – Socio-economic Realities*. ISBN 81-7141-524-3.

Vol. 4 *HIV/AIDS – Law Ethics and Human Rights*, 2 Parts. ISBN 81-7141-526-1.

Vol. 5 *AIDS and NGOs*. ISBN 81-7141-527-X.

Vol. 6 *AIDS and Home Care*. ISBN 81-7141-528-8.

Vol. 7 *STD Case Management*. ISBN 81-7141-529-6.

Vol. 8 *HIV/AIDS Prevention and Care – Teaching Modules for Nurses and Midwives*. ISBN 81-7141-530-X.

Vol. 9 *HIV Prevention Education for Educational Institutions*. ISBN 81-7141-531-8.

Vol. 10 *Instructional Modules for AIDS Education*. ISBN 81-7141-532-6.

Vol. 11 *School Health Education to Prevent AIDS and STD – A Package for Curriculum Planners*. ISBN 81-7141-533-4.

Bhaskara Rao, Digumarti, Editor (2000). *International Encyclopaedia of Human Rights*, 7 Volumes in 13 Parts. New Delhi: Discovery Publishing House. ISBN 81-7141-567-9 (set).

Vol. 1 *International Instruments of Human Rights*, 2 Parts. ISBN 81-7141-569-4.

Vol. 2 *Regional Instruments of Human Rights*. ISBN 81-7141-604-7.

Vol. 3 Human Rights and the United Nations, 2 Parts. ISBN 81-7141-605-5.

Vol. 4 *Fact Files of Human Rights*, 3 Parts. ISBN 81-7141-606-3.

Vol. 5 *Study Stories of Human Rights*, 3 Parts. ISBN 81-7141-607-3.

Vol. 6 *International Meetings on Human Rights*, 2 Parts. ISBN 81-714-608-X.

Vol. 7 *Professional Training in Human Rights*. ISBN 81-7141-609-8.

Bhaskara Rao, Digumarti, Editor (2000). *International Encyclopaedia of Science and Technology Education*, 11 Volumes. New Delhi: Discovery Publishing House. ISBN 81-7141-548-2 (set).

Vol. 1 *Science and Technology Education*. ISBN 81-7141-568-7.

Vol. 2 *Science Education in Developing Countries*. ISBN 81-7141-569-9.

Vol. 3 *Organizational Structure of Science*. ISBN 81-7141-570-9.

Vol. 4 *Science Education in Asia and the Pacific*. ISBN 81-7141-571-7.

Vol. 5 *Science and Technology Education For All*. ISBN 81-7141-572-5.

Vol. 6 *Values, Ethics, Talent and Girls in Science and Technology Education*. ISBN 81-7141-573-3.

Vol. 7 *Popularisation of Science and Technology Education*. ISBN 81-7141-574-1.

Vol. 8 *Science, Power and Society*. ISBN 81-7141-575-X.

Vol. 9 *Information Technology*. ISBN 81-7141-576-8.

Vol. 10 *Teacher Training in Science and Technology Education*. ISBN 81-7141-577-6.

Vol. 11 *Teacher Training in Science and Technology: A Curriculum Framework*. ISBN 81-7141-578-4.

Bhaskara Rao, Digumarti, Editor (2000). *Education For All: Achieving the Goal*, 3 Volumes. New Delhi: APH Publishing Corporation. ISBN 81-7648-152-1 (set).

Vol. I *The Global Consensus*. ISBN 81-7648-155-6.

Vol. II *Mid-Decade Review Reports of Regional Seminars*. ISBN 81-7648-154-8.

Vol. III Issues and Trends. ISBN 81-7648-155-6.

Bhaskara Rao, Digumarti, Editor (2001). *Nuclear Materials: Issues and Concerns*, 2 Volumes. New Delhi: Discovery Publishing House. ISBN 81-7141-611-X.

Bhaskara Rao, Digumarti, Editor (2001). *Distance Education in Different Countries*. New Delhi: APH Publishing Corporation. ISBN 81-7648-229-3.

Bhaskara Rao, Digumarti, Editor (2001). *Decentralised Management of Education: Management of Education in Panchayati Raj and Municipal Bodies*. New Delhi: Discovery Publishing House. ISBN 81-7141-617-9.

Bhaskara Rao, Digumarti, Editor (2001). *Electrochemistry for Environmental Protection*. New Delhi: Discovery Publishing House. ISBN 81-7141-619-5.

Bhaskara Rao, Digumarti, Editor (2001). *Global Educational Studies*. New Delhi: Discovery Publishing House. ISBN 81-7141-616-0.

Bhaskara Rao, Digumarti, Editor (2001). *Global Synthesis of Educational Assessment*. New Delhi: Discovery Publishing House. ISBN 81-7141-613-6.

Bhaskara Rao, Digumarti, Editor (2001). *Jomtein Decade of Education*. New Delhi: Discovery Publishing House. ISBN 81-7141-618-7.

Bhaskara Rao, Digumarti, Editor (2001). *World Conference on Education for All*. New Delhi: Discovery Publishing House. ISBN 81-7141-274-9.

Bhaskara Rao, Digumarti, Editor (2001). *World Conference on Higher Education*. New Delhi: Discovery Publishing House. ISBN 81-7141-610-1.

Bhaskara Rao, Digumarti, Editor (2001). *World Conference on Science*. New Delhi: Discovery Publishing House. ISBN 81-7141-612-8.

Bhaskara Rao, Digumarti, Editor (2003). *Inspiring Experiences in Teacher Education*. New Delhi: Discovery Publishing House. ISBN 81-7141-656-X.

Bhaskara Rao, Digumarti, Editor (2003). *International Studies in Education*, 3 Volumes. New Delhi: Discovery Publishing House. ISBN 81-7141-647-0.

Bhaskara Rao, Digumarti, Editor (2003). *Military Conversion: Impact on Science and Technology.* New Delhi: Discovery Publishing House. ISBN 81-7141-578-4.

Bhaskara Rao, Digumarti, Editor (2003). *United Nations Millennium Summit.* New Delhi: Discovery Publishing House. ISBN 81-7141-632-2.

Bhaskara Rao, Digumarti, Editor (2003). *World Assembly on Aging.* New Delhi: Discovery Publishing House. ISBN 81-7141-637-3.

Bhaskara Rao, Digumarti, Editor (2003). *World Conference on Human Rights.* New Delhi: Discovery Publishing House. ISBN 81-7141-661-6.

Bhaskara Rao, Digumarti, Editor (2003). *World Education Forum.* New Delhi: Discovery Publishing House. ISBN 81-7141-639-X.

Bhaskara Rao, Digumarti, Editor (2003). *Education, Employment and Human Resource Development.* New Delhi: Discovery Publishing House. ISBN 81-7141-681-0.

Bhaskara Rao, Digumarti, Editor (2003). *Successful Schooling.* New Delhi: Discovery Publishing House. ISBN 81-7141-677-2.

Bhaskara Rao, Digumarti, Editor (2003). *European Education and Teachers.* New Delhi: Discovery Publishing House. ISBN 81-7141-702-7.

Bhaskara Rao, Digumarti, Editor (2003). *Teachers in a Changing World.* New Delhi: Discovery Publishing House. ISBN 81-7141-694-2.

Bhaskara Rao, Digumarti, Editor (2004). *International Guidelines on Open and Distance Teacher Education.* New Delhi: Discovery Publishing House. ISBN 81-7141-777-9.

Bhaskara Rao, Digumarti, Editor (2004). *Adult Learning in the 21st Century.* New Delhi: Discovery Publishing House. ISBN 81-7141-797-3.

Bhaskara Rao, Digumarti, Editor (2004). *Educational Practices: Research and Recommendations.* New Delhi: Discovery Publishing House. ISBN 81-7141-835-X.

Bhaskara Rao, Digumarti, Editor (2004). *General Secondary Education In the 21st Century.* New Delhi: Discovery Publishing House. ISBN 81-7141-885-6.

Bhaskara Rao, Digumarti, Editor (2004). *International Encyclopaedia of Learning to Live Together*, 4 Volumes. New Delhi: Discovery Publishing House. ISBN 81-7141-848-1.

Vol. 1 *International Conference on Learning to Live Together.*

Vol. 2 *Globalisation and Living Together.*

Vol. 3 *Curriculum for Learning to Live Together.*

Vol. 4 *Science Education for the Contemporary Society.*

Bhaskara Rao, Digumarti, Editor (2004). *Reforming Secondary Education.* New Delhi: Discovery Publishing House. ISBN 81-7141-843-0.

Bhaskara Rao, Digumarti, Editor (2004). *Human Rights Education.* New Delhi: Discovery Publishing House. ISBN 81-7141-882-1.

Bhaskara Rao, Digumarti, Editor (2004). *United Nations Decade for Human Rights Education.* New Delhi: Discovery Publishing House. ISBN 81-7141- 887-2.

Bhaskara Rao, Digumarti, Editor (2004). *Technical and Vocational Education and Training in the 21st Century.* New Delhi: Discovery Publishing House. ISBN 81-7141-984-4.

Bhaskara Rao, Digumarti, Editor (2005). *Encyclopaedia of Education For All*, 5 Volumes. New Delhi: Discovery Publishing House.

Bhaskara Rao, Digumarti and B.S.V. Dutt, Editors (2003). *Education: Programmes and Policies.* New Delhi: APH Publishing Corporation. ISBN 81-7648-470-9.

Bhaskara Rao, Digumarti, C.A.P. Swamy and B.S.V. Dutt (1997). *Self-Evaluation in Student Teaching.* New Delhi: Discovery Publishing House. ISBN 81-7141-374-9.

Bhaskara Rao, Digumarti and D. Naresh Kumar (2004). *School Teacher Effectiveness.* New Delhi: Discovery Publishing House. ISBN 81-7141-782-5.

Bhaskara Rao, Digumarti and D. Sridhar (2002). *Job Satisfaction of School Teachers.* New Delhi: Discovery Publishing House. ISBN 81-7141-652-7.

Bhaskara Rao, Digumarti, C. Sridevi and K. Vijaya (1995). *Achievement in Social Studies*. New Delhi: Discovery Publishing House. ISBN 81-7141-281-5.

Bhaskara Rao, Digumarti and Digumarti Pushpa Latha (1994). *Achievement in Biology*. New Delhi: Discovery Publishing House. ISBN 81-7141-264-5.

Bhaskara Rao, Digumarti and Digumarti Pushpa Latha (1995). *Achievement in English*. New Delhi: Discovery Publishing House. ISBN 81-7141-283-1.

Bhaskara Rao, Digumarti and Digumarti Pushpa Latha (1994). *Achievement in Science*. New Delhi: Discovery Publishing House. ISBN 81-7141-280-70.

Bhaskara Rao, Digumarti and Digumarti Pushpa Latha (1995). *Achievement in Mathematics*. New Delhi: Discovery Publishing House. ISBN 81-7141-278-5.

Bhaskara Rao, Digumarti and Digumarti Pushpa Latha (2004). *Education for Women*. New Delhi: Discovery Publishing House. ISBN 81-7141-873-2.

Bhaskara Rao, Digumarti, Digumarti Pushpa Latha and Digumarthi Harshitha, Editors (2001). *Biological Warfare*. New Delhi: Discovery Publishing House. ISBN 81-7141-597-0.

Bhaskara Rao, Digumarti, Digumarti Pushpa Latha and Digumarthi Harshitha, Editors (2001). *Women as Educators*. New Delhi: Discovery Publishing House. ISBN 81-7141-602-0.

Bhaskara Rao, Digumarti and Digumarthi Harshitha (2004). *Adjustment of Adolescents*. New Delhi: APH Publishing House. ISBN 81-7648-836-8.

Bhaskara Rao, Digumarti and Digumarthi Harshitha, Editors (2001). *Education in India*. New Delhi: APH Publishing House. ISBN 81-7648-207-2.

Bhaskara Rao, Digumarti and Digumarti Pushpa Latha, Editors (1998). *International Encyclopaedia of Women*, 5 Volumes. New Delhi: Discovery Publishing House. ISBN 81-7141-410-9 (set).

Vol. 1 *Status of World's Women*. ISBN 81-7141-494-X.

Vol. 2 *Women, Education and Empowerment*. ISBN 81-7141-498-1.

Vol. 3 *Women Challenges and Advancement*. ISBN 81-7141-497-4.

Vol. 4 *Women and Family Health*. ISBN 81-7141-497-4.

Vol. 5 *Women and International Action*. ISBN 81-7141-498-2.

Bhaskara Rao, Digumarti, Digumarti Pushpa Latha and Digumarthi Harshitha, Editors (2001). *Assessing Learning Achievement*. New Delhi: Discovery Publishing House. ISBN 81-7141-601-2.

Bhaskara Rao, Digumarti, Digumarti Pushpa Latha and Digumarthi Harshitha, Editors (2001). *Energy Security*. New Delhi: Discovery Publishing House. ISBN 81-7141-598-9.

Bhaskara Rao, Digumarti, Digumarthi Harshitha and K.R.S. Sambasiva Rao, Editors (1999). *Advanced Biotechnology*. New Delhi: Discovery Publishing House. ISBN 81-7141-516-4.

Bhaskara Rao, Digumarti and K.R.S. Sambasiva Rao, editors (1996). *Current Trends in Indian Education*. New Delhi: Discovery Publishing House. ISBN 81-7141-311-0.

Bhaskara Rao, Digumarti and E. Sreekanth Babu (2004). *Educational Interests of School Students*. New Delhi: Discovery Publishing House. ISBN 81-7141-837-6.

Bhaskara Rao, Digumarti and K. Vijaya (1995). *A Text Book Evaluation*. Ambala Cantt: The Associated Publishers.

Bhaskara Rao, Digumarti and M.A. Fayaz (2004). *Problems of Primary School Drop-outs*. New Delhi: Discovery Publishing House. ISBN 81-7141-834-1.

Bhaskara Rao, Digumarti and N.V.M. Mohana Rao (2002). *Problems of Mentally Handicapped Children*. New Delhi: Discovery Publishing House. ISBN 81-7141-645-4.

Bhaskara Rao, Digumarti and S. Chandra Mohan (2002). *Sports Management*. New Delhi: APH Publishing House. ISBN 81-7648-467-9.

Bhaskara Rao, Digumarti and S.A. Khader (2004). *Problems of Private School Teachers*. New Delhi: Discovery Publishing House. ISBN 81-7141-838-4.

Bhaskara Rao, Digumarti and S.A. Khader (2004). *School Education in India*. New Delhi: Discovery Publishing House. ISBN 81-7141-849-X.

Bhaskara Rao, Digumarti and Sk. Johni Basha (2004). *Teachers' Population Education Awareness*. New Delhi: Discovery Publishing House. ISBN 81-7141-832-5.

Bhaskara Rao, Digumarti, V.V. Rao, V.V. Lakshmi and V.V. Krishna, Editors (1999). *Status and Advancement of Women*. New Delhi: APH Publishing Corporation. ISBN 81-7648-169-6.

Appala Naidu, P.Ch., Author and Digumarti Bhaskara Rao, Editor (2007). *Feedback Methods and Student Performance*. New Delhi: Discovery Publishing House. ISBN 81-8356-284-1.

Babu, P.C., Author and Digumarti Bhaskara Rao, Editor (2004). *Flowers of Wisdom*. New Delhi: Discovery Publishing House. ISBN 81-7141-695-0.

Bujji Babu, K., Author and Digumarti Bhaskara Rao, editor (2007). *Teaching Aptitude of Primary School Teachers*. New Delhi: Sonali Publications. ISBN 81-8411-083-9.

Amala, P.A. and Anupama, P., Authors and Digumarti Bhaskara Rao, Editor (2004). *History of Education*. New Delhi: Discovery Publishing House. ISBN 81-7141-860-0.

Bhagya Lakshmi, L., Author and Digumarti Bhaskara Rao, Editor (2000). *Reading and Comprehension*. New Delhi: Discovery Publishing House. ISBN 81-7141-543-1.

Bhasha, S.A., Author and Digumarti Bhaskara Rao, Editor (2004). *Methods of Teaching Geography*. New Delhi: Discovery Publishing House. ISBN 81-7141-807-4.

Bhuvaneswara Lakshmi, Gadde, Author and Digumarti Bhaskara Rao, Editor(2000). *Attitude Towards Science*. New Delhi: Discovery Publishing House. ISBN 81-7141-541-6.

Bhuvaneswara Lakshmi, G., Author and Digumarti Bhaskara Rao, Editor (2004). *Methods of Teaching Life Science*. New Delhi: Discovery Publishing House. ISBN 81-7141-804-X.

Bhuvaneswara Lakshmi, G. and K. Subba Rao, Authors and Digumarti Bhaskara Rao, Editor (2004). *Methods of Teaching Biology*. New Delhi: Discovery Publishing House. ISBN 81-7141-914-3.

Bramhaiah, T., Author and Digumarti Bhaskara Rao, Editor (2008). *Stress of Prospective Teachers*. New Delhi: Sonali Publications.

Chary, K.V.N.B., Author and Digumarti Bhaskara Rao, Editor (2006). *Techniques of Teaching Physics*. New Delhi: Sonali Publications. ISBN 81-8411-046-4.

Chowdary, S.B.J.R. and Naga Raju, Authors and Digumarti Bhaskara Rao, Editor (2004). *Mastery of Teaching Skills*. New Delhi: Discovery Publishing House. ISBN 81-7141-861-9.

Dayakara Reddy, V. and Digumarti Bhaskara Rao, Editors (2006). *Value-oriented Education*. New Delhi: Discovery Publishing House. ISBN 81-8356-051-2.

Devraj, T.A.S., Author and Digumarti Bhaskara Rao, Editor (1997). *Trace Analysis of Uranium and Thorium*. New Delhi: Discovery Publishing House. ISBN 81-7141-375-7.

Durga Rani, K., Author and Digumarti Bhaskara Rao, Editor (2000). *Educational Aspirations and Scientific Attitudes*. New Delhi: Discovery Publishing House. ISBN 81-7141-555-5.

Dutt, B.S.V. and Digumarti Bhaskara Rao (2001). *Empowering Primary Teachers*. New Delhi: Discovery Publishing House. ISBN 81-7141-615-2.

Dutt, B.S.V., Author and Digumarti Bhaskara Rao, Editor (2004). *Comparative Education*. New Delhi: Discovery Publishing House. ISBN 81-7141-912-7.

Ediger, Marlow and Digumarti Bhaskara Rao (1996). *Science Curriculum*. New Delhi: Discovery Publishing House. ISBN 81-7141-321-8.

Ediger, Marlow and Digumarti Bhaskara Rao (2000). *Teaching Mathematics Successfully*. New Delhi: Discovery Publishing House. ISBN 81-7141-552-0.

Ediger, Marlow and Digumarti Bhaskara Rao (2001). *Teaching Science Successfully*. New Delhi: Discovery Publishing House. ISBN 81-7141-600-4.

Ediger, Marlow and Digumarti Bhaskara Rao (2001). *Teaching Social Studies Successfully*. New Delhi: Discovery Publishing House. ISBN 81-7141-596-2.

Ediger, Marlow and Digumarti Bhaskara Rao (2002). *Philosophy and Curriculum*. New Delhi: Discovery Publishing House. ISBN 81-7141-631-4.

Ediger, Marlow and Digumarti Bhaskara Rao (2002). *Improving School Administration*. New Delhi: Discovery Publishing House. ISBN 81-7141-633-0.

Ediger, Marlow and Digumarti Bhaskara Rao (2002). *Elementary Curriculum*. New Delhi: Discovery Publishing House. ISBN 81-7141-658-6.

Ediger, Marlow and Digumarti Bhaskara Rao (2003). *Language Arts Curriculum*. New Delhi: Discovery Publishing House. ISBN 81-7141-657-8.

Ediger, Marlow and Digumarti Bhaskara Rao (2003). *Psychology and Curriculum*. New Delhi: Discovery Publishing House. ISBN 81-7141-691-8.

Ediger, Marlow and Digumarti Bhaskara Rao (2003). *Teaching Language Arts Successfully*. New Delhi: Discovery Publishing House. ISBN 81-7141-678-0.

Ediger, Marlow and Digumarti Bhaskara Rao (2003). *School Curriculum and Administration*. New Delhi: Discovery Publishing House. ISBN 81-7141-709-4.

Ediger, Marlow and Digumarti Bhaskara Rao (2003). *Teaching Mathematics in Elementary Schools*. New Delhi: Discovery Publishing House. ISBN 81-7141-687-X.

Ediger, Marlow and Digumarti Bhaskara Rao (2003). *Teaching Science in Elementary Schools*. New Delhi: Discovery Publishing House. ISBN 81-7141-698-5.

Ediger, Marlow and Digumarti Bhaskara Rao (2003). *School Curriculum and Administration*. New Delhi: Discovery Publishing House. ISBN 81-7141-709-4.

Ediger, Marlow and Digumarti Bhaskara Rao (2003). *Elementary Curriculum Improvement*. New Delhi: Discovery Publishing House. ISBN 81-7141-740-X.

Ediger, Marlow and Digumarti Bhaskara Rao (2004). *School Organisation*. New Delhi: Discovery Publishing House. ISBN 81-7141-843-0.

Ediger, Marlow and Digumarti Bhaskara Rao (2004). *Relevancy in Elementary Curriculum*. New Delhi: Discovery Publishing House. ISBN 81-7141-845-9.

Ediger, Marlow and Digumarti Bhaskara Rao (2005). *Quality School Education*. New Delhi: Discovery Publishing House. ISBN 81-8356-022-9.

Ediger, Marlow and Digumarti Bhaskara Rao (2006). *Successful School Education*. New Delhi: Discovery Publishing House. ISBN 81-8356-054-7.

Ediger, Marlow and Digumarti Bhaskara Rao (2006). *Successful School Administration*. New Delhi: Discovery Publishing House. ISBN 81-8356-046-6.

Ediger, Marlow and Digumarti Bhaskara Rao (2006). *Issues in School Curriculum*. New Delhi: Discovery Publishing House. ISBN 81-8356-052-0.

Ediger, Marlow and Digumarti Bhaskara Rao (2006). *Community College – Curriculum and Teaching*. New Delhi: Discovery Publishing House. ISBN 81-8356-053-9.

Ediger, Marlow and Digumarti Bhaskara Rao (2006). *Administration of Schools*. New Delhi: Discovery Publishing House. ISBN 81-8356-244-2

Ediger, Marlow and Digumarti Bhaskara Rao (2006). *Reading Curriculum and Instruction*. New Delhi: Discovery Publishing House. ISBN 81-8356-266-3.

Ediger, Marlow and Digumarti Bhaskara Rao (2006). *Curriculum Organisation*. New Delhi: Discovery Publishing House. ISBN 81-8356-205-1.

Ediger, Marlow and Digumarti Bhaskara Rao (2006). *Curriculum of School Subjects*. New Delhi: Discovery Publishing House. ISBN 81-8356-207-8.

Ediger, Marlow, B.S.V. Dutt and Digumarti Bhaskara Rao (2003). *Teaching English Successfully*. New Delhi: Discovery Publishing House. ISBN 81-7141-707-8.

Ediger, Marlow and Digumarti Bhaskara Rao (2007). *School Science Education*. New Delhi: Discovery Publishing House. ISBN 81-8356-352-X.

Ediger, Marlow and Digumarti Bhaskara Rao (2007). *Language Arts Education*. New Delhi: Discovery Publishing House. ISBN 81-8356-333-3.

Elizabeth, M.E.S., Author and Digumarti Bhaskara Rao, Editor (2004). *Methods of Teaching English*. New Delhi: Discovery Publishing House. ISBN 81-7141-809-0.

Elizabeth, M.E.S., Author and Digumarti Bhaskara Rao, Editor (2004). *Acquisition of English Vocabulary*. New Delhi: Discovery Publishing House. ISBN 81-8356-075-X.

Fatima, Sk. Author and Digumarti Bhaskara Rao, Editor (2007). *Reasoning Ability of School Students*. New Delhi: Discovery Publishing House. ISBN 81-8356-330-9.

Fatima, Sk. and Digumarti Bhaskara Rao (2008). *Reasoning Ability of Adolescent Students*. New Delhi: Discovery Publishing House. ISBN 978-81-8356-31-4

Gopala Krishna, M., Author and Digumarti Bhaskara Rao, Editor (2007). *Techniques of Teaching Physical Education*. New Delhi: Sonali Publications. ISBN 81-8411-044-8.

Gopala Krishna, M., Author and Digumarti Bhaskara Rao, Editor (2007). *Techniques of Teaching Education*. New Delhi: Sonali Publications. ISBN 81-8411-062-6.

Harshitha, Digumarthi, Author and Digumarti Bhaskara Rao, Editor (2004). *Methods of Teaching Information Technology*. New Delhi: Discovery Publishing House. ISBN 81-7141-805-8.

Harshitha, Digumarthi, Author and Digumarti Bhaskara Rao, Editor (2007). *Techniques of Teaching Computer Science*. New Delhi: Sonali Publications. ISBN 81-8411-036-7.

Indira Devi, Author and J. Prasanth Kumar and Digumarti Bhaskara Rao, Editors (2004). *Values in Language Text Books*. New Delhi: Discovery Publishing House. ISBN 81-7141-833-3.

Jalaja Kumari, C., Author and Digumarti Bhaskara Rao, Editor (2004). *Methods of Teaching Educational Technology*. New Delhi: Discovery Publishing House. ISBN 81-7141-810-4.

Jalaja Kumari, C., Author and Digumarti Bhaskara Rao, Editor (2007). *Job Satisfaction of Teachers*. New Delhi: Discovery Publishing House. ISBN 81-8356-329-5.

Janardhan Reddy, B., Author and Digumarti Bhaskara Rao, Editor (2006). *Techniques of Teaching Sociology*. New Delhi: Sonali Publications. ISBN 81-8411-042-1.

Jayalakshmi, M., Author and Digumarti Bhaskara Rao, Editor (2008). *Microteaching and Prospective Teachers*. New Delhi: Sonali Publications.

Jayasree, K., Author and Digumarti Bhaskara Rao, Editor (1999). *Correlates of Socialisation*. New Delhi: Discovery Publishing House. ISBN 81-7141-517-2.

Jayasree, K., Author and Digumarti Bhaskara Rao, Editor (2004). *Methods of Teaching Science*. New Delhi: Discovery Publishing House. ISBN 81-7141-801-5.

John Babu, C., Author and T.J.R. Prasad, G.M. Madhukar and Digumarti Bhaskara Rao, Editors (2004). *Problem Solving in Mathematics*. New Delhi: APH Publishing Corporation. ISBN 81-7648-273-0.

Joseph Raju, B and G.A. Anitha, Authors and Digumarti Bhaskara Rao, Editor (2004). *Population Education*. New Delhi: Sonali Publications. ISBN 81-88836-31-3.

Lalitha, T., Author and K.S. Prabhakaram, D.S.N. Sastry and Digumarti Bhaskara Rao, Editors (2004). *Educational Philosophic Beliefs*. New Delhi: Discovery Publishing House. ISBN 81-7141-765-5.

Krishna, G., Author and Digumarti Bhaskara Rao, Editor (2006). *Techniques of Teaching Physical Education*. New Delhi: Sonali Publications. ISBN 81-8411-044-8.

Kumar Raja, G., Author and Digumarti Bhaskara Rao, Editor (2007). *Principles of Primary School*. New Delhi: Sonali Publications. ISBN 81-8411-054-5.

Lakshmi Kumari, V., Author and Digumarti Bhaskara Rao, Editor (2006). *Techniques of Teaching Home Science*. New Delhi: Sonali Publications. ISBN 81-8411-048-0.

Madhava, K., Author and Digumarti Bhaskara Rao, Editor (2008). *Personality of Adolescent Students*. New Delhi: Discovery Publishing House. 978-81-8356-262-1.

Madhu Bala, Jampala, Author and Digumarti Bhaskara Rao, Editor (2004). *Methods of Teaching Exceptional Children*. New Delhi: Discovery Publishing House. ISBN 81-7141-802-3.

Madhu Bala, Jampala, Author and Digumarti Bhaskara Rao, Editor (2007). *Adjustment Problems of Hearing Impaired*. New Delhi: Discovery Publishing House. ISBN 81-7141-831-7.

Marja, Talvi and Digumarti Bhaskara Rao, Editors (1996). *Educational Leadership and Social Changes*. New Delhi: Discovery Publishing House. ISBN 81-7141-320-X.

Mohana Sundari, C., Author and B. Prasad Babu and Digumarti Bhaskara Rao, Editors (2008). *Stress Among Pregnant Women* New Delhi: Discovery Publishing House. 978-81-8356-316-1.

Naga Kumari, U., Author and Digumarti Bhaskara Rao, Editor (2008). *Science Process Skills of School Students*. New Delhi: Discovery Publishing House. ISBN 978-81-8356-263-8.

Nageswara Rao, S. and M. Srihari, Authors and Digumarti Bhaskara Rao, Editor (2004). *Guidance and Counselling*. New Delhi: Discovery Publishing House. ISBN 81-7141-840-6.

Nageswara Rao, S., Author and Digumarti Bhaskara Rao, Editor (2006). *Techniques of Teaching Psychology.* New Delhi: Sonali Publications. ISBN 81-8411-040-5.

Nageswara Rao, S. and P. Sridhar, Authors and Digumarti Bhaskara Rao, Editor (2004). *Methods and Techniques of Teaching.* New Delhi: Sonali Publications. ISBN 81-88836-33-8.

Nirmala Jyothi, M., Author and Digumarti Bhaskara Rao, Editor (2003). *Non-detention System in School Education.* New Delhi: Discovery Publishing House. ISBN 81-7141-654-3.

Padma Tulasi, G., Author and Digumarti Bhaskara Rao, Editor (2004). *Methods of Teaching Elementary Science.* New Delhi: Discovery Publishing House. ISBN 81-7141-871-6.

Pala Prasada Rao, V., Author and K.N. Rani and D. Bhaskara Rao, Editors (2004). *India-Pakistan: Partition Perspectives in Indo-English Novels.* New Delhi: Discovery Publishing House. ISBN 81-7141-871-6.

Pala Prasada Rao, V., Author and D. Bhaskara Rao, Editors (2008). *Functioning of Autonomous Colleges.* New Delhi: Discovery Publishing House. ISBN 978-81-8356-258-4.

Pitchi Reddy, M., Author and Digumarti Bhaskara Rao, Editor (2007). *Techniques of Teaching Social Sciences.* New Delhi: Sonali Publications. ISBN 81-8411-066-X.

Prasad Babu, B., Author and P. Madhu and Digumarti Bhaskara Rao, Editors (2006). *Psychological Adjustment and Well-being.* New Delhi: Discovery Publishing House. ISBN 81-8356-204-3.

Prasad Babu, B., Author and M.V.R. Raju and Digumarti Bhaskara Rao, Editors (2006). *Behavioural Problems of School Children.* New Delhi: Discovery Publishing House. ISBN 81-8356-206-X.

Prabhakaram, K.S., Author and Digumarti Bhaskara Rao, Editors (1998). *Concept Attainment Model in Mathematics Teaching.* New Delhi: Discovery Publishing House. ISBN 81-7141-424-9.

Prasanth Kumar, J., Author and Digumarti Bhaskara Rao, Editor (1998). *Effectiveness of Distance Education System.* New Delhi: Discovery Publishing House. ISBN 81-7141-437-0.

Prasanth Kumar, J., Author and Digumarti Bhaskara Rao, Editor (2004). *Methods of Teaching Civics*. New Delhi: Discovery Publishing House. ISBN 81-7141-806-6.

Prasanth Kumar, J., Author and G. Sundara Rao and Digumarti Bhaskara Rao, Editors (2000). *Open University Student Support Services*. New Delhi: Discovery Publishing House. ISBN 81-7141-550-4.

Raja Kumari, M.A. and D.R.S. Sundari, Authors and Digumarti Bhaskara Rao, Editor (2004). *Special Education*. New Delhi: Discovery Publishing House. ISBN 81-7141-846-5.

Raja Kumari, M.A. and D.R.S. Sundari, Authors and Digumarti Bhaskara Rao, Editor (2004). *Methods of Teaching Educational Psychology*. New Delhi: Discovery Publishing House. ISBN 81-7141-820-1.

Rajeswari, S. M., Author and T. Santhanam, B. Prasad Babu and Digumarti Bhaskara Rao, Editors (2008). *Stress and Attitude of Women Teachers*. New Delhi: Discovery Publishing House. ISBN 978-81-8356-324-6.

Ramatulasamma, K., Author and Digumarti Bhaskara Rao, Editor (2002). *Job Satisfaction of Teacher Educators*. New Delhi: Discovery Publishing House. ISBN 81-7141-655-1.

Rama Krishnaiah, D., Author and Digumarti Bhaskara Rao, Editor (1998). *Job Satisfaction of College Teachers*. New Delhi: Discovery Publishing House. ISBN 81-7141-438-9.

Rama Kumar Ratnam, M.V., Author and Digumarti Bhaskara Rao, Editor (1998). *Dukkha: Suffering in Early Buddhism*. New Delhi: Discovery Publishing House. ISBN 81-7141-653-5.

Rama Krishna Prasad and P. Vide Sagar, Authors and Digumarti Bhaskara Rao, Editor (2004). *Methods of Teaching Physical Education*. New Delhi: Discovery Publishing House. ISBN 81-7141-868-6.

Rama Seshaiah, P. Author and Digumarti Bhaskara Rao, Editor (2004). *Methods of Teaching Home Science*. New Delhi: Discovery Publishing House. ISBN 81-7141-916-X.

Rama Swamy, K., Author and Digumarti Bhaskara Rao, Editor (2007). *Techniques of Teaching Environmental Science*. New Delhi: Sonali Publications. ISBN 81-8411-035-9.

Ramesh, A.R., Author and Digumarti Bhaskara Rao, Editor (2006). *Techniques of Teaching Commerce*. New Delhi: Sonali Publications. ISBN 81-8411-043-X.

Ramesh, Ghanta and Digumarti Bhaskara Rao, Editors (1998). *Environmental Education: Problems and Prospects*. New Delhi: Discovery Publishing House. ISBN 81-7141-423-0.

Ranga Rao, B., Author and Digumarti Bhaskara Rao, Editor (2007). *Techniques of Teaching Economics*. New Delhi: Sonali Publications. ISBN 81-8411-056-1.

Ranga Rao, R., Author and Digumarti Bhaskara Rao, Editor (2004). *Methods of Teacher Teaching*. New Delhi: Discovery Publishing House. ISBN 81-7141-812-0.

Rani, S.S., Author and Digumarti Bhaskara Rao, Editor (2006). *Techniques of Teaching Botany*. New Delhi: Sonali Publications. ISBN 81-8411-037-5.

Rathaiah, Lavu and Digumarti Bhaskara Rao, Editors (1996), *International Innovations in Education*. New Delhi: Discovery Publishing House. ISBN 81-7141-359-5.

Rathaiah, Lavu and Digumarti Bhaskara Rao (1997). *Achievement Correlates*. New Delhi: Discovery Publishing House. ISBN 81-7141-385-4.

Ravi Krishna, M., Author and Digumarti Bhaskara Rao, Editor (2004). *Examination System*. New Delhi: Discovery Publishing House. ISBN 81-7141-824-4.

Ravi Kumar, M., Author and Digumarti Bhaskara Rao, Editor (2004). *Methods of Teaching Computer Science*. New Delhi: Discovery Publishing House. ISBN 81-7141-823-6.

Roja Ramani, V., Author and Digumarti Bhaskara Rao, Editor (2009). *Frustration of Prospective Teachers*. New Delhi: Discovery Publishing House.

Rudramamba, B., Author and Digumarti Bhaskara Rao, Editor (2003). *Problems of Teaching*. New Delhi: APH Publishing Corporation. ISBN 81-7648-462-8.

Rudramamba, B. and V. Lakshmi Kumari, Authors and Digumarti Bhaskara Rao, Editor (2004). *Methods of Teaching Economics*. New Delhi: Discovery Publishing House. ISBN 81-7141-900-3.

Sambasiva Rao, P., Author and Digumarti Bhaskara Rao, Editor (2007). *Techniques of Teaching Psychology*. New Delhi: Sonali Publications. ISBN 81-8411-040 5.

Sanjeeva Rao, P.C., Author and Digumarti Bhaskara Rao, Editor (1996). *A Text Book of Geology*. New Delhi: Discovery Publishing House. ISBN 81-7141-313-7.

Santhanam, T., B. Prasad Babu and S. Sugandhi, Authors and Digumarti Bhaskara Rao, Editor (2007). *Children with Learning Disabilities*. New Delhi: Sonali Publications. ISBN 81-8411-077-4.

Santhanam, T., B. Prasad Babu and S. Sugandhi, Authors and Digumarti Bhaskara Rao, Editor (2008). *Learning Disabilities and Remedial Programmes*. New Delhi: Discovery Publishing House. ISBN 978-81-8356-257-7.

Sarala, M.M.O., Author and Digumarti Bhaskara Rao, Editor (2006). *Techniques of Teaching English*. New Delhi: Sonali Publications. ISBN 81-8411-047-2.

Satya Narayana, G., Author and Digumarti Bhaskara Rao, Editor (2008). *Attitude Towards Social Studies and Achievement in Social Studies*. New Delhi: Discovery Publishing House. ISBN 978-81-8356-261-4.

Satya Narayana, V., Author and Digumarti Bhaskara Rao, Editor (2001). *Physical Education, Social Attitudes and Leadership Qualities*. New Delhi: Discovery Publishing House. ISBN 81-7141-593-8.

Satya Narayana, P.V.V. and G. Krishna, Authors and Digumarti Bhaskara Rao, Editor (2004). *Curriculum Development and Management*. New Delhi: Discovery Publishing House. ISBN 81-7141-813-9.

Shamsuddin, Sk. and V. Dayakara Reddy, Authors and Digumarti Bhaskara Rao, Editor (2007). *Value and Academic Achievement*. New Delhi: Discovery Publishing House. ISBN 81-8356-283-3.

Singh, Y.C., Author and Digumarti Bhaskara Rao, Editor (2006). *Techniques of Teaching Science*. New Delhi: Sonali Publications. ISBN 81-8411-041-3.

Sirisha Rani, S., Author and Digumarti Bhaskara Rao, Editor (2007). *Techniques of Teaching Botany*. New Delhi: Sonali Publications. ISBN 81-8411-037-5.

Sivaratnam Reddy, M., Author and Digumarti Bhaskara Rao, Editor (2004). *Creativity in College Students*. New Delhi: Discovery Publishing House. ISBN 81-7141-697-7.

Siva Lakshmi, G.V. and G.L. Subbaiah, Authors and Digumarti Bhaskara Rao, Editor (2004). *Methods of Teaching Environmental Science*. New Delhi: Discovery Publishing House. ISBN 81-7141-839-2.

Srinivas, G. and Digumarti Bhaskara Rao (2007). *Anxiety of Prospective Teachers*. New Delhi: Sonali Publications. ISBN 81-8411-084-7.

Srinivas, M. and I. Prasada Rao, Authors and Digumarti Bhaskara Rao, Editor (2004). *Methods of Teaching History*. New Delhi: Discovery Publishing House. ISBN 81-7141-803-1.

Srinivas Rao, P., Author and Digumarti Bhaskara Rao, Editor (2007). *Principles of Secondary School*. New Delhi: Sonali Publications. ISBN 81-8411-058-8.

Srinivasulu Reddy, M. and K.R.S. Sambasiva Rao, Authors and Digumarti Bhaskara Rao, Editor (1999). *A Text Book of Aquaculture*. New Delhi: Discovery Publishing House. ISBN 81-7141-482-6.

Srinivasa Rao, Mandalapu, Author and Digumarti Bhaskara Rao, Editor (2003). *Achievement Motivation and Achievement in Mathematics*. New Delhi: Discovery Publishing House. ISBN 81-7141-674-8.

Srihari, M., Author and Digumarti Bhaskara Rao, Editor (2003). *Values of Prospective Teachers*. New Delhi: Discovery Publishing House. ISBN 81-8356-328-7.

Subba Rao, K., Author and Digumarti Bhaskara Rao, Editor (2007). *School Education Policy*. New Delhi: Discovery Publishing House. ISBN 81-8356-285-X.

Subba Rao, K., Author and Digumarti Bhaskara Rao, Editor (2007). *Educational Planning*. New Delhi: Sonali Publications. ISBN 81-8411-053-7.

Sudhakar Reddy, Y., Author and Digumarti Bhaskara Rao, Editor (2003). *Creativity in Adolescents*. New Delhi: Discovery Publishing House. ISBN 81-7141-659-4.

Sunil Kumar, K. and K. Rama Krishana, Authors and Digumarti Bhaskara Rao, Editor (2004). *Methods of Teaching Chemistry*. New Delhi: Discovery Publishing House. ISBN 81-7141-913-5.

Suneetha, G., Author and Digumarti Bhaskara Rao, Editor (2004). *Environmental Awareness of School Students*. New Delhi: Sonali Publications. ISBN 81-8411-085-5.

Sunita, E. and R. Sambasiva Rao, Authors and Digumarti Bhaskara Rao, Editor (2004). *Methods of Teaching Mathematics*. New Delhi: Discovery Publishing House. ISBN 81-7141-915-1.

Suresh, K., Author and Digumarti Bhaskara Rao, Editor (2008). *Social Intelligence of Prospective Teachers*. New Delhi: Sonali Publications.

Surya Madhava, I., Author and Digumarti Bhaskara Rao, Editor (2006). *Techniques of Teaching Geography*. New Delhi: Sonali Publications. ISBN 81-8411-034-0.

Surya Madhava, I., Author and Digumarti Bhaskara Rao, Editor (2007). *Techniques of Teaching Political Science*. New Delhi: Sonali Publications. ISBN 81-8411-061-8.

Suvarna Raju, T.J.M., Author and M.V.R. Raju, B. Prasad Babu and Digumarti Bhaskara Rao, Editors (2008). *Personality and Adjustment of University Hostel Students*. New Delhi: Sonali Publications.

Swamy, K.R., Author and Digumarti Bhaskara Rao, Editor (2006). *Techniques of Teaching Environmental Science*. New Delhi: Sonali Publications. ISBN 81-8411-035-9.

Swarna Jyothi, K., Author and Digumarti Bhaskara Rao, Editor (2007). *Educational Research*. New Delhi: Sonali Publications. ISBN 81-8411-063-4.

Swarna Latha, C.D., and Digumarti Bhaskara Rao, Editors (2006). *Encyclopaedia of Biotechnology*, 5 Volumes. New Delhi: Discovery Publishing House. ISBN 81-8356-168-3.

Swarupa Rani, T. and J.R. Priyadarshini, Authors and Digumarti Bhaskara Rao, editor (2004). *Educational Measurement and Evaluation*. New Delhi: Discovery Publishing House. ISBN 81-7141-859-7.

Vanaja, M., Author and Digumarti Bhaskara Rao, Editor (1999). *Inquiry Training Model*. New Delhi: Discovery Publishing House. ISBN 81-7141-515-6.

Vanaja, M., Author and Digumarti Bhaskara Rao, Editor (2004). *Methods of Teaching Physics*. New Delhi: Discovery Publishing House. ISBN 81-7141-867-8.

Valeri V. Koustiouk, Author and Digumarti Bhaskara Rao, Editor (2002). *A Text Book of Cryogenics*. New Delhi: Discovery Publishing House. ISBN 81-7141-642-X.

Vamsi Krishna, V., Author and Digumarti Bhaskara Rao, Editor (2004). *School Psychology*. New Delhi: Discovery Publishing House. ISBN 81-7141-880-5.

Veena Kumari, Balusu and Digumarti Bhaskara Rao (1996). *Operation Black Board*. New Delhi: APH Publishing Corporation. ISBN 81-7024-711-X.

Veena Kumari, Balusu, Author and Digumarti Bhaskara Rao, Editor (2004). *Methods of Teaching Social Studies*. New Delhi: Discovery Publishing House. ISBN 81-7141-899-6.

Veena Kumari, Balusu, Author and Digumarti Bhaskara Rao, Editor (2000). *Psycho-Social Correlates of Achievement*. New Delhi: Discovery Publishing House. ISBN 81-7141-547-4.

Venkata Rao, B., Author and Digumarti Bhaskara Rao, Editor (2007). *Techniques of Teaching Chemistry*. New Delhi: Sonali Publications. ISBN 81-8411-057-X.

Venkata Rao, P. and Digumarti Bhaskara Rao (1989). *A Text Book of Zoology – Junior Intermediate*. Guntur: Vignan Publishers.

Venkata Rao, P. and Digumarti Bhaskara Rao (1989). *A Text Book of Zoology – Senior Intermediate*. Guntur: Vignan Publishers.

Venkateswara Rao, V., Author and Digumarti Bhaskara Rao, Editor (2004). *Problems of Education*. New Delhi: Discovery Publishing House. ISBN 81-7141-841-4.

Venkateswara Rao, V., V. Vijaya Lakshmi and V. Vamsi Krishna, Authors and Digumarti Bhaskara Rao, Editor (2004). *Education For All*. New Delhi: Sonali Publications. ISBN 81-88836-30-3.

Venkateswara Rao, V., V. Vijaya Lakshmi and V. Vamsi Krishna, Authors and Digumarti Bhaskara Rao, Editor (2004). *Education in India*. New Delhi: Sonali Publications. ISBN 81-88836-858-9.

Venkateswara Reddy, L. and Narayana, M. L., Authors and Digumarti Bhaskara Rao, Editor (2004). *Education for Dalits*. New Delhi: Discovery Publishing House. ISBN 81-7141-872-4.

Venkateswara Reddy, L. and Narayana, M. L, Authors and Digumarti Bhaskara Rao, Editor (2004). *Methods of Teaching Rural Sociology*. New Delhi: Discovery Publishing House. ISBN 81-7141-811-2.

Venkateswarlu, K. and S.J. Basha, Authors and Digumarti Bhaskara Rao, Editor (2004). *Methods of Teaching Commerce*. New Delhi: Discovery Publishing House. ISBN 81-7141-808-2.

Venugopala Rao, K., Author and Digumarti Bhaskara Rao, Editor (2000). *Teacher Morale in Secondary Schools*. New Delhi: Discovery Publishing House. ISBN 81-7141-551-2.

Venugopala Rao, K., Author and Digumarti Bhaskara Rao, Editor (2007). *Techniques of Teaching History*. New Delhi: Sonali Publications. ISBN 81-8411-059-6.

Vidya, C., Author and Digumarti Bhaskara Rao, Editor (1996). *A Text Book of Nutrition*. New Delhi: Discovery Publishing House. ISBN 81-7141-309-9.

Vimala, T.D., B. Prasad Babu and Digumarti Bhaskara Rao, Editors (2007). *Stress, Coping and Management*. New Delhi: Sonali Publications. ISBN 81-8411-086-3.

Vijaya Bharathi, D., Author and Digumarti Bhaskara Rao, Editor (2000). *Educational Philosophies of Swami Vivekananda and John Dewey*. New Delhi: APH Publishing House. ISBN 81-7648-309-9.

Vijaya Bharathi, D., Author and Digumarti Bhaskara Rao, Editor (2005). *Educational Philosophy of John Dewey*. New Delhi: Discovery Publishing House. ISBN 81-8356-024-5.

Vijaya Bharathi, D., Author and Digumarti Bhaskara Rao, Editor (2005). *Educational Philosophy of Swami Vivekananda*. New Delhi: Discovery Publishing House. ISBN 81-8356-023-7.

Vijaya Lakshmi, D., Author and Digumarti Bhaskara Rao, Editor (2004) *Basic Education*. New Delhi: Discovery Publishing House. ISBN 81-7141-881-3.

Vijaya Lakshmi, V., Author and Digumarti Bhaskara Rao, Editor (2006). *Techniques of Teaching Music*. New Delhi: Sonali Publications. ISBN 81-8411-038-3.

Vijaya Kumar, S.J., Author and Digumarti Bhaskara Rao, Editor (2006). *Techniques of Teaching Mathematics*. New Delhi: Sonali Publications. ISBN 81-8411-039-1.

Visalakshi, V., Author and Digumarti Bhaskara Rao, Editor (2006). *Techniques of Teaching Biology*. New Delhi: Sonali Publications. ISBN 81-8411-045-6.

Visalakshi, V., Author and Digumarti Bhaskara Rao, Editor (2007). *Techniques of Teaching Zoology*. New Delhi: Sonali Publications. ISBN 81-8411-055-3.

Books in Telugu Language

Bhaskara Rao, Digumarti (1986). *Dhrushya Sravana Bodhanapakaranalu* (Audio Visual Teaching Aids). Guntur: Nagarjuna Publishers.

Bhaskara Rao, Digumarti (1993). *Jeevasasthra Bodhana* (Teaching of Biology). Guntur: Nagarjuna Publishers.

Bhaskara Rao, Digumarti (1995). *Vignanasasthra Bodhana* (Teaching of Science) Guntur: Nagarjuna Publishers.

Bhaskara Rao, Digumarti (1997). *Vidya Manovignana Sasthram* (Educational Psychology). Guntur: Creative Press.

Bhaskara Rao, Digumarti (1998). *DSC Study Material*. Guntur: Nagarjuna Publishers.

Bhaskara Rao, Digumarti (1998). *Upadhyayudu Vidya*. (Teacher and Education) Guntur: Nagarjuna Publishers.

Bhaskara Rao, Digumarti (1998). *Vidya Drukpadalu* (Perspectives of Education). Guntur: Nagarjuna Publishers.

Bhaskara Rao, Digumarti (1999). *EdCET Teaching Aptitude*. Guntur: Nagarjuna Publishers.

Bhaskara Rao, Digumarti (2001). *Bharata Samajamulo Upadyayudu Vidhya* (Teacher and Education in Emerging Indian Society). Guntur: Sri Nagarjuna Publishers.

Bhaskara Rao, Digumarti (2001). *Bhoutika Sasthra Bodhana Padhatulu* (Methods of Teaching Physical Science). Guntur: Sri Nagarjuna Publishers.

Bhaskara Rao, Digumarti (2001). *Jeeva Sasthra Bodhana Padhatulu* (Methods of Teaching Biology).Guntur: Sri Nagarjuna Publishers.

Bhaskara Rao, Digumarti (2001). *Vidya Manovignana Sasthram* (Educational Psychology). Guntur: Sri Nagarjuna Publishers.

Bhaskara Rao, Digumarti (2003). *Patasala Yajamanyam/Paripalana* (School Management and Administration). Guntur: Sri Nagarjuna Publishers.

Gopala Krishna, G., A. Rama Krishna, K. Subba Rao and Bhaskara Rao, Digumarti (2004). *Jeevasasthra Bodhana Padhatulu* (Methods of Teaching of Biological Science). Guntur: Sri Nagarjuna Publishers.

Krishna Murthy, V., K.S. Sudheer Reddy and Digumarti Bhaskara Rao (2004). *Vidya Manovignana Sasthra Adharalu* (Foundations of Educational Psychology). Guntur: Sri Nagarjuna Publishers.

Lalini, V., V. Dayakara Reddy, M. Srihari and Digumarti Bhaskara Rao (2004). *Vidya Adharalu* (Foundations of Education). Guntur: Sri Nagarjuna Publishers.

Subba Rao, K.P., P. Ayodhya and Digumarti Bhaskara Rao (2004). *Patasala Yajamanyam – Vidhya Vyavasthalu* (School Management and Systems of Education). Guntur: Sri Nagarjuna Publishers.

Sudhakar, V., B. Ravindra Babu, D.S. Kumar and Digumarti Bhaskara Rao (2004). *Vidya Sanketika Sasthram — Computer Vidhya* (Educational Technology and Computer Education). Guntur: Sri Nagarjuna Publishers.

Index

A

ACS Summer Teaching Workshop, 12
Administrative difficulty, 87
Advantages of microteaching, 81, 85
Aggarwal, J.C., 14, 80, 83
Aids and apparants in microteaching, 81
Allen, Dwight W., 14, 18
Analysis of data, 127-132
Ananthakrishan, N., 85
Anticipatory set, 38
Assumptions of microteaching,
  expanding knowledge of results, 55-56
  focus on training, 55
  increased control of practice, 55
  real teaching, 55
  reduced complexities, 55

B

Babu, Ram, 14, 16, 86
Be yourself, dont try to fake it, 30
Bhagwan, Verma, 106
Bishnu, Charan Das, 108
Blank form for hunter model, 47
Briefing stage, 90
Brown, 65

C

CASE, 61
Centre for Astrophysics, 95
Characteristics of microteaching, 54
Chatley, Y.P., 108
Checking for understanding, 39
China, 18
Clift, J.C., 15
Closing stage, 73
Closure, 39, 73
Concept of microteaching, 4
  scaled-down teaching encounter, 5

D

Das, R.C., 110
Debriefing stage, 91
Definitions of key terms, 120
  attitude, 121
  educational qualification, 121
  gender, 121
  locality, 121
  methodology, 121
  microteaching, 121
  prospective teachers, 121
  study, 120
Derek Bok Centre for Teaching and Learning, 17
Dont apologise, 30
Dve, La, 15
Dyson, Sam, 96

E

Educational implications, 9

Educational qualification, 122
Effective lecturing, 43
    consideration of the audience, 43
    illustrative devices, 44
    personality of the lecturer, 43
    planning and organisation, 43
    preparation of the audience, 43
    repetition, 44
    time length, 44
    varied stimuli, 44
    vocabulary, 43
Encyclopaedia of Education, 15
Evaluation for microteaching-6, 52
Evaluation instruments, 80

F

Fagen, Adam, 94
Foschi, Silvia, 99

G

Gandhi, K.V., 110
Gender, 122, 135
Gor, K.V., 110
Graduate and postgraduate prospective teachers, 138
Guided practice, 39
Guidelines for preparation for a good microteaching, 92

H

Hypotheses of the study, 123

I

Improvement of microteaching, 88
Independent practice, 39
Indian Model of Microteaching, 61
Input and modeling, 39
Introduction, 1-9

J

Jangira, N.K., 15, 16
Johnson, Olivia, 95
Joshi, 65

K

Knight, M.C., 15
Know your audience, 29
Know your material, 29
Knowledge acquisition phase, 59
Kulshreshta, S.P., 110
Kumar, K.L., 85, 88
Kumar, Yogendra, 106

L

Limitations of microteaching
    costly, 86
    difficulty in actual practice, 86
    disturbs existing time-table, 86
    narrow scope, 86
    presentation in parts, 86
Locality, 122
Location, 135
Look sharp and expect butterflies, 29

M

Madeline Hunter Mastery Teaching, 47
Make use of visual aids, 29
Male and female prospective teachers, 137
Marc Scheff, Junior in Computer Science, 92
Materials for microteaching, 40
    lesson plans, 40
    microteaching, 40
    things to think about, 40
Matto, Jangira, 107
Medium of instruction, 122
Medium of instruction, 135
Menon, 65
Methodology, 122

Microteaching and
achievement, 110
anxiety, 110
attitude, 114
block teaching practice,. 108
classroom behaviour, 118
direct or indirect behaviour, 117
effectiveness of microteaching, 108
feedback, 100
gender, 106
intelligence, 104
locality, 106
modeling, 113
personality, 103
qualifications, 106
self concept, 103
teacher behaviour, 118
teaching competence, 111
– methodology, 107
– skills, 64, 104
traditional teaching, 56
awareness, 56
duration, 56
pattern of classroom interaction, 56
practicing skill, 56
providing feedback, 56
role of supervisor, 56
score, 56
simple versus complex teaching, 56
size of class, 56
specifications of objectives, 56
verbal behaviour, 117
Microteaching skills, 6
Microteaching, 3
Miltza, 16
Model of microteaching, 61
Modern categories of basic skills in teaching
developing pupil thinking, 79
evaluation skills, 79
managerial skills, 79
motivation skills, 78
planning skills, 78
presentation skills, 78
questioning skills, 78
skill of small group instruction, 78
Murthy, S.K., 60

N

NCERT, 61
Need of the study, 7
NTTCHP, 89

O

Objective, 38, 57
Outline your talk in advance, 29

P

Pandiane, Chanzdur C., 106, 108
Pandya, M.J., 106, 110
Passi, B.K., 65
Peer supervision, 19
Practice your presentation, 29
Pratap, D., 108
Preparation stage, 90
Pre-reading activity, 51
Presentation stage, 72
Principles underlying in microteaching
class management, 76
completeness of communication, 78
divergent questions, 77
explaining, 75

fluency in questioning, 74
giving assignment, 76
illustration and use of examples, 75
increasing pupil participation, 75
lecturing, 77
pacing the lesson, 77
planned repetition, 78
principle of continuity, 63
– – evaluation, 63
– – experimentation, 63
– – practices, 62
– – precise supervision, 63
– – reinforcement, 62-63
probing questions, 74
recognizing and attending behaviour, 74
reinforcing pupil participation, 74
teacher silence and non-verbal cues, 74
use of higher order questions, 77
using audio-visual aids, 76
– blackboard, 75-76
writing instructional objectives. 76

Procedure of microteaching, 58
defining the skill, 58
demonstrating the skills, 58
discussion, 58
planning the lesson, 58
re-discussion, 59
repeating the cycle, 59
re-planning, 58
re-teaching, 59
teaching the lesson, 58

Prospective teachers posses a high attitude towards microteaching, 136

Q

Qualification, 135

R

Rao, Usha, 1, 2
Reason its importance, 39
Research methodology, 120-126
Results and discussion, 89
Review of related literature, 10-119
concept attainment model, 40
evaluation, 41
explanation, 32
feedback, 30-31
how to micro-teach, 17-18
instruction, 24
introduction, 24-25
little red riding hood, 32-36
materials for microteaching-1, 22
meaning of microteaching, 13-16
methods, 41
microteaching, 38-39
– courses, 21-22
– models of teaching skills, 21
new micro-teaching simplified, 18-20
objective, 41
observation guide for your initial visit to your mentor teachers classroom, 22
performing in front of others, 28-30
rationale, 40
round table troubles, 37-38
self-evaluation for microteaching, 39
set induction, 25-28
student presentations. 28
students, 23

teacher, 23-24
teaching writing, 36-38
theoretical perspectives, 11-13
things to think about, 25
things to think about, 32
variants of microteaching, 20-21
what to prepare, 18
why microteaching, 16-17
Role of supervisor in microteaching
developing ability to perform a skill, 79
evaluating the lesson, 80
making understanding the application of skill, 79
supervising the lesson, 80
visiting schools, 79-80
working with trainees, 79
Ross, Elizabeth, 98
Rural and Durban prospective teachers, 137

S

Sample of the study, 123
Science and arts prospective teachers, 138
Self-evaluation, 49, 51
Self-study groups, 19
Set induction, 73
Sharma, R.N., 79
Show interest in your topic, 29
Singh, Jangira, 107
Skill acquisition phase, 59
Statement of the problem, 7
Stimulus variation, 73
Student examples
anticipatory set, 48
checking students understanding and guided practice, 49
closure, 49
independent practice, 49
input and modeling, 49
motivation, 48
objectives, 48
Suggestions for further research, 139
Summative evaluation, 53

T

Teach/reteach stage, 90
Teacher education programme, 2
Teacher, 27
Teaching fellows talk about microteaching, 92
Teaching methodology, 135
Teaching skills, 2, 65, 66, 67, 68, 69, 70, 71
Telugu medium and English medium perspective teachers, 138
Things to think about, 52
Tool of the study, 125
Transfer phase, 59
Turney, 16
Two + two evaluation protocol, 19

U

Uses of the lecture, 42
to change the pace, 42
-- convey enthusiasm, 42
-- convey information, 42
-- inform students of expected results, 42
- reinforce written work, 42
-- synthesis many sources, 42

V

Variables of the study, 122
Verma, Bhagwan, 108
Viewing and analysis of sessions, 91

W

Williams, T., 48

□□□